JEAN-CLAUDE GRUMBERG: THREE PLAYS

T0163497

EXPLORING JEWISH ARTS AND CULTURE
ROBERT H. ABZUG, SERIES EDITOR
Director of the Schusterman Center for Jewish Studies

Jews in the realms of the arts and culture have imagined extraordinary worlds and shaped dominant cultures in ways that are only now being fully recognized and studied. The books in this series, produced by established scholars and artists, will further this revelation and make substantive contributions to both scholarly and public understandings of art, drama, literature, photography, film, dance, music, foodways, cultural studies, and other expressions of humanity as filtered through the Jewish experience, both secular and religious.

THREE PLAYS

Jean-Claude Grumberg

Translated and Introduced by Seth L. Wolitz

University of Texas Press ◆ AUSTIN

The Workplace: Original title: *L'Atelier*, © Papiers 1985, ACTES SUD 1999

On the Way to the Promised Land: A Dental Tragedy: Original title: *Vers toi terre promise: Une tragédie dentaire*, © ACTES SUD 2006

Mama's Coming Back, Poor Orphan: Original title: *Maman revient, pauvre orphelin*, © ACTES SUD 1994

"Interview with Jean-Claude Grumberg," in "Le Dossier" presented by Anne Cassou-Nogues and Marie-Aude de Langenhagen in *L'Atelier*, Jean-Claude Grumberg © Flammarion, coll. Etonnants Classiques for presentation, notes, chronology, and record, 2006. © Actes Sud for the original edition, 1979.

Requests for permission to reproduce material from this work should be sent to:
   Permissions
   University of Texas Press
   P.O. Box 7819
   Austin, TX 78713–7819
   http://utpress.utexas.edu/index.php/rp-form

⊛ The paper used in this book meets the minimum requirements of ANSI/NISO Z39.48-1992 (R1997) (Permanence of Paper).

Library of Congress Control Number: 2014935917

ISBN: 978-0-292-75455-3 (cloth : alk. paper)
ISBN: 978-0-292-75458-4 (pbk. : alk. paper)
doi:10.7560/754553

Contents

Acknowledgments *vii*

Three French Jewish Plays of Jean-Claude Grumberg:
A Theatre of Memory and Accommodation *1*

Jean-Claude Grumberg:
A Timeline of Key Works and Life Events *21*

The Plays
> *The Workplace 29*
> *On the Way to the Promised Land: A Dental Tragedy 107*
> *Mama's Coming Back, Poor Orphan 157*

An Interview with Jean-Claude Grumberg *175*

Selected Bibliography *183*

Acknowledgments

A work of art constructed of words in a single language re-quires an interpretation in another language no less demanding than a fine musician giving sound to the recorded notes on a com-poser's score. A translator is not only an interpreter but also one who must seek to make the literary work resound with as much esthetic success as the original. One has only to consider the bril-liant metamorphosis of verse by Edgar Allen Poe put into French by Baudelaire and Mallarmé or Shakespeare's plays rekindled in Ger-man by Schlegel. I cannot even pretend to approach such perfec-tion. I should be happy if my own efforts in translating these three Grumberg plays garner some critical appreciation. One task that I faced in translating these plays from French to English, aside from seeking the accuracy of equivalent meaning and nuances, was to find the style and tone that captured the distinct popular Parisian registers in which Grumberg shaped his characters in their verbal dress.

I found in sharing my translation efforts with the critical eyes of colleagues and friends that I often incorporated their suggestions and improvements, enriching the translation and bringing it closer to the esthetic intent of the original. I cannot conceive of a better reader than Michael Ochs, whose editing eye and superb ear for col-loquial English massively helped me improve the manuscript. Nor can I thank enough the readings of Michael Nimetz, Dan Aynes-worth, Jean-Pierre Cauvin, Charles Mackey, and the poet/translator Leonard Wolf, whose patient readings and cautious advice were both useful and fruitful in enriching the translations. For any inadequacies of my translation, of course, I am fully responsible.

I should also like to acknowledge the help of my close Parisian friend, Charles Baron, who belongs to this world of Parisian Jewry that experienced bitterly the Occupation, deportation, and inadequate restoration after the war and whose powerful memory and wonderful knowledge of now-dated Parisian argot helped me to understand many nuances of the text that needed a colorful American idiomatic equivalent.

Jean-Claude Grumberg proved to be not only a wonderful dramatist but over time a good friend who shared with me in his Parisian apartment many of the realities he faced in creating these plays: the sources of many scenes, his political and cultural perspectives, his sense of history, the seriousness of art to express the human condition, and experiences in his own life that led to their esthetic translation.

I should especially like to express my appreciation to Robert Abzug, professor of history and American studies as well as the director of the Schusterman Center for Jewish Studies at the University of Texas at Austin, who suggested and encouraged the translations of Grumberg's plays as proof of a vital expression of contemporary European Jewish cultural life. I am honored to find a place in his new series on Exploring Jewish Arts and Culture being published by the University of Texas Press.

The support and encouragement of the University of Texas Press over the years has been continuous. I cannot thank sufficiently the insights and good words of Jim Burr and the editorial labors of Leslie Tingle and her staff in the shaping of this volume.

This volume of plays owes much to my wife, Louise Berman Wolitz, to whom I dedicate this translation. She encouraged my work and came up with some of the truly idiomatic phrases I incorporated in the text.

SETH L. WOLITZ

Three French Jewish Plays of Jean-Claude Grumberg

A Theatre of Memory and Accommodation

I

Jean-Claude Grumberg (1939–) succeeds as no one else before him in placing on the French stage authentic contemporary Jews, ordinary French Parisian Jews speaking contemporary French rich in slang and sounding totally normal, expressing their daily thoughts and cares, stresses and obsessions in calm, boisterous, timid, or humorous language. Here they are, the survivors of a recent genocide, giggling, sharing jokes, or mourning over their lost ones, getting on in life, banal people, some muted, some with chips on their shoulders, working away, worrying about their children or pensions and dreaming of utopias. None content. French to the tips of their fingers and yet Jews, too, made more consciously Jewish by the war and yellow stars sewn on their clothes. Their presence on stage is a challenge: We're here! We're back! Did you miss us? You, who denounced us to the police? Or did you really miss us, genuinely? Are we at home again? We're in a new chapter, right? A new Republic, the Fifth Republic, *Vive la France*! Grumberg's theatre captures the aftermath of Vichy and the Shoah and their effect upon contemporary France and its citizens, Jewish and Gentile.

The three prize-winning plays presented here form a natural trilogy of Grumberg's French Jewish works of the last forty years: *The Workplace* (*L'Atelier*, 1979), *On the Way to the Promised Land: A*

Jean-Claude Grumberg, by Frédéric Nauczyciel

Dental Tragedy (*Vers toi terre promise: Une tragédie dentaire*, 2006), and *Mama's Coming Back, Poor Orphan* (*Maman revient, pauvre orphelin*, 1994). They are presented in historical chronology, rather than in the year of their creation, so we may appreciate more strongly these plays as documentary witnesses of the post-war era, a central esthetic position of Grumberg. The plays follow the immediate post-war reality up to the end of the twentieth century steeped in the author's personal experience and insights into contemporary Parisian life. The playwright appears in all three plays as a character from early childhood until his "retirement," permitting the audience both autobiographical and generational perspectives on the events presented in each play. These plays and their performance create a *lieu de mémoire* (a site of memory) for a generation that has few physical vestiges of the past. The plays are like historical plaques placed on the theatre, marking dark events and the refusal to allow them historical oblivion.

The theme of re-integration into French life therefore permeates all three plays and underlines the awkwardness, if not discomfort, of being a French citizen of Jewish origin accommodating back to a world one considered once one's own and from which one was rejected to the point of annihilation. How does one become "at home" in contemporary France? The Shoah appears strictly as a memory trace but affects sotto voce present-day choices of action and being. Grumberg's trilogy focuses on the art of accommodation, the skills needed to be "forward looking" and holding the past at bay. These plays therefore register the aftermath of the Shoah leading consistently forward into contemporary life.

Grumberg, a student of Molière, constructs these three French Jewish plays making use of humor—dark humor pitched with steep irony—to bring out the truth of humans trapped both in an uncaring society and their own foibles. Humor teases the audience to recognize the bitter truths of their own human condition and why, then, the characters, no different from themselves, must act as they do. Humor in fact brings three-dimensional life to the characters, insists on their humanity and ordinariness, and makes the pain of even their post-war condition understandable and bearable to both a Gentile and Jewish audience. Grumberg creates empathy through humor and unexpected insights. The very laughter of the audience can boomerang on itself as it realizes suddenly that the comic moment actually veils a life-or-death situation. The use of humor is probably Grumberg's most astonishing achievement in treating the lugubrious condition of French Jewry in mid-century Europe.

Grumberg's French Jewish plays are not Holocaust plays but interpretations of post-war French Jewish life, the aftermath of genocide, in the second part of the twentieth century, when the crucial disaster of World War II affected every Frenchman and European, but especially the Jews. Grumberg's French Jewish plays are there-

fore markers of the psychological states and conditions of both Jewish and non-Jewish Frenchmen in the evolving new reality of a
France shorn of its prestige, power, and empire and yet not fully
ready to come to terms with its Vichy past. Grumberg's trilogy and
his other plays contribute to the exposure of this repressed past of
the war and depict the little known or appreciated lives of ordinary
French Jewish survivors who, in Samuel Beckett's terms, "I can't
go on, I must go on." Grumberg's plays are therefore very European plays, and his perspective is that of a contemporary European
French Jew.

II

Grumberg belongs to the generation of European Jewish playwrights born either before World War II or just after who reflect
both the national experience of their country of birth or of choice
and the particular experience of European Jewry that was the Shoah
and its aftermath. This generation has produced a new European
theatrical experience: hybrid plays in the national tongue that quietly assert a Jewish presence as part of the national inheritance.
Whether Harold Pinter (1930–2008), Sir Arnold Wesker (1930–),
and Bernard Kops (1926–) in the United Kingdom, Georg Tabori
(1914–2007) in German lands, or Michel Vinaver (né Grinberg,
1927–), Gilles Ségal (1932–), and Jean-Claude Grumberg (1939–) in
France, among the most notable dramatists, their plays reflect new
perspectives and esthetic expressions interpreting the European and
Jewish experiences that are distinct from the Jewish American or
Israeli experience of these freighted years. Unlike the Yiddish and
Hebrew theatre, which reaches a single audience of Jewish speak-
ers, these playwrights must work with a dual audience of Gentiles
and Jews in the majority language of the country and reach both
groups attending the play. This condition creates a hybrid theatre, in
which allusions and interpretations permit double entendre and in-

sights that can be appreciated by the entire audience or certain allusions that can only be picked up by one side. The plays therefore are European—appealing at once to both the Jewish and the indigenous majority—and national, according to the language used on stage.

Grumberg's performative art stands in full contrast with his slightly older contemporary, Marcel Marceau (1923–2007), stage name of Marcel Mangel, the Strasbourg Jew who fled his city and survived in the Free Zone owing to his masquerading skills. After World War II, he became the greatest mime of the twentieth century. He chose silence to depict his experiences and vision of the world, universalizing the human condition embodied in what in Yiddish was known as *dos pintele yid*, the ordinary ne'er-do-well poor exilic Jew, by creating his alter ego, Bip the Clown (akin to Charlie Chaplin's Tramp), who cannot verbalize what he knows and feels—language has failed him. He depends instead on silence and gesture to plumb the depths of his life's experience (and of his generation), which he shares through the mediation of pantomime. His *mimodrame La Cage* [The Cage] is the perfect mimicry of the era he experienced as physical and spiritual entrapment—as in a concentration camp—with its snuffing out of a life in an ever-reducing space. This powerful and horrific silence reflects the condition of mid-century despair, and it is echoed especially in the character of Lucky in Beckett's *Waiting for Godot* (1953). Against the pervasive silence, melancholia, and universalizing of Marcel Marceau's mime theatre (employed as well by Gilles Ségal—a disciple who performed with the mime master—in his theatre with remarkable salience), Grumberg's stage ruminates and roars with living sound, people who are alive, normal, ordinary people using speech, the most human form of expression. Grumberg demands words, language, verbal gestures: grunts; whines; murmurs; utterance fully oral with natural delivery passing from ferocious intensity, shouts, and threats to whispered fears; unfinished sentences declaring unendurable concerns; moanings, tears; and sudden eruptions of boisterous laughter, mixing chatter and nonsense confused with harsh truths and double meanings. Grumberg's theatre captures the hour and the minute of a believable ordinary being admirable in the determination to talk, complain, laugh, and go on. Marcel Marceau's Bip survives, and Grumberg's sentient characters plunge into life wanting to enjoy it, fully aware of their vulnerable living presence—miraculous—against the lurid past. Both artists share the same generational experiences: loss of their fathers to deportation and death, flight from their hometowns and family, and the tensions of being Jews during the Occupation and creating a post-war meaningful existence. But each expresses in his own medium a different interpretation. Marceau uses *l'art du silence* to express the inexpressible in language, placing all his talent in gesture, producing resonant silence,[1] whereas Grumberg, also an actor, exploits language, character, and social events to project the universal in the particular utterance.

From Grumberg's perspective, the past teaches nothing, the future appears ill defined. The present is all you have, and "You Could Live If They Let You" (to quote the title of the comic novelist Wallace Markfield's 1974 book). Verbal intensity and particularly the use of slang mixed with much humor signal Grumberg's profile in his theatre, and he shares this quality with the leading contemporary Jewish playwright in German, Georg Tabori. European Jewish theatre is intensely verbal, and Grumberg's plays reflect that need of the living to be heard, to express themselves: speaking means being alive. The European Jewish theatre does not believe that silence is golden, it means either death or stupidity. Or perhaps just fear? European Jewish theatre is a subaltern theatre. It is a minority theatre in a dominant language culture of which it partakes; thus it is hybridic theatre, esthetically successful in fusing the two cultures.

---

1. "The people who came back from the [concentration] camps were never able to talk about it. My name is Mangel. I am Jewish. Perhaps that, unconsciously, contributed towards my choice of silence" (Marceau, quoted at the Internet Movie Database [www.imdb.com], in the biography).

III

The emergence of French Jewish theatre is a comparatively late development in French cultural domains. France was the first nation in Europe to extend full citizenship to the Jews of France in 1791. This event implied from the French perspective the abandonment of any extra-territorial allegiances and consequently full loyalty to the French Republic. The state also recognized the legitimacy of a Jewish religious identity. Frenchmen of Jewish origin throughout the nineteenth century participated fully in French cultural manifestations strictly as Frenchmen in what they believed to be French universal culture. In French theatre the artists and dramatists of Jewish origin were committed to French ideals and full cultural assimilation. Rachel and Sarah Bernhardt, both of Jewish origin, committed to French classics and new plays, performing as French actresses, and dismissed allusions to their origins from negative critics. French opera embraced Jews native and foreign like Giacomo Meyerbeer (1791–1864), Jacques Halévy (1799–1862), and Jacques Offenbach (1819–1880), who helped create nineteenth-century Paris as the center of grand opera and the opéra comique. Halévy's tragic opera *La Juive* [The Jewish woman] (1835) was seen, not as a Jewish cultural expression, but rather as a tragedy of religious bigotry—Catholic and Jewish—that French Enlightenment culture scorned with the secular Republican values of *liberté, égalité, fraternité* in exactly the same fashion that Meyerbeer's opera *Les Hugenots* [The Hugenots] (1836) denounced the massacres of Protestants on Saint Bartholomew's Day.

In the latter part of the nineteenth and early twentieth century, particularly in the popular *théâtre de boulevard*, Parisian conventional theatre (comparable to Broadway plays in America or the West End theatre in London) performed the very successful plays of Georges de Porto-Riche (1849–1930), Gaston de Caillavet (1870–1915), Tristan Bernard (1866–1947), Henri Bernstein (1876–1953), and even today's Yasmina Reza (1959–), all Frenchmen of Jewish origin. Like David Belasco, S. N. Behrman, Georges Kaufmann, and Moss Hart on Broadway, French playwrights of Jewish origin expressed the ideals and spirit of the national culture and eschewed treating Jewish topics or creating Jewish characters. Their commitment was to French secular cultural values of the Republic, and their identity was, to use the words of the historian Marc Bloch, murdered by the Germans, "Civis Gallicum Sum" (I am a citizen of France).

The Dreyfus Affair of 1892–1899 and the traumatic experience of Occupied France in World War II, 1940–1944, however, questioned the place of French Jewry in the body politic. Up to World War II, French Jewry sought and indeed participated as ordinary Frenchmen in the universal values trumpeted by the French Republic and certainly in its brilliant culture. But Vichy deprived Jews of their civil rights and made all Jews stateless, following the example of Nazi Germany.

The experience of the Shoah and its aftermath left French Jewry reeling. Of the 330,000 Jews in France in 1940, 75,721 were deported. Only 2,654 returned alive. In France during the war they had to wear the yellow star, were restricted in their movements, were not permitted to practice their professions, were deprived often of their homes and possessions, and were continuously harassed and threatened with deportation. Hiding and using false papers were their best hope of survival. The war left serious psychic wounds. While some argued that these experiences should be put away and that French Jews should join again as before in the French commonweal, other Jews felt that their experience was so affecting that they needed to express their experience and new perspective as a minority voice in French cultural life.

Despite the reluctance of the post-war Gaullist government to call into question the history of Vichy's participation in the extermination of French Jewry, French Jews and others began publishing memoirs, historical studies, and—inevitably in esthetic modes—poems, novels, and finally drama. The cinema played an important role as well, revealing Vichy collaboration and full participation in the deportation of French Jewry, particularly Louis Malle's *Lacombe, Lucien* (1973); the famous documentary *Le Chagrin et La Pitié* [*The Sorrow and the Pity*] (1969), directed by Marcel Ophüls; and *Shoah* (1985), directed by Claude Lanzmann.

The treatment of the Shoah on stage emerged comparatively late owing to subtle pressures by the government to bury the subject. The first treatment of the French Jewish experience during the war occurred when Arthur Miller's play *Incident at Vichy* was approved for production in 1964. Soon after the events of 1968 brought the end to the Gaullist era, the subjects of World War II, including Vichy and the Jews, became open to serious discourse. The Paul Touvier case (1972–1973), involving a Vichy official who was hidden in a Catholic abbey for years and was implicated in the murder of Jews, electrified France, for he was the first and only Frenchman convicted of perpetrating crimes against humanity at that time. These events finally opened the French stage to treating the Jewish experience—but set elsewhere, not yet France. Jean-Claude Grumberg was the first to show violent anti-Semitism and allude to the Shoah in his play *Dreyfus* (1974), set in Poland in 1930, in which amateur Jewish actors are preparing a play about Captain Dreyfus when some Polish anti-Semitic ruffians violently invade the rehearsal and beat up the actors. The idealistic director decides to go off to a civilized place: Berlin, 1933! The play, performed at the prestigious Odéon Théâtre in Paris, slyly alludes to French anti-Semitism placed back in time to the Dreyfus Affair but foreshadowing the Shoah with Polish anti-Semitic violence and the irony of thirties Berlin as an ideal. This play marks the beginning of French Jewish theatre, in which the author treats French Jewish concerns from the perspective of a French Jew, a citizen of France, and with a minority perspective. This play was quickly followed by many new French Jewish playwrights treating the Shoah in their works, including Paul Kraemer (1938–), Liliane Atlan (1932–2011), Victor Haim (1935–), Gilles Ségal (1932–), and René Kalisky (1936–1981). These dramatists were of the same generation who grew up during wartime as young children, and its effect shaped their worldview.

They received a full French education, and they hold a full cultural attachment to their homeland that is their own, but they have a definite Jewish consciousness without any religious affiliation. Their dramas reflect this condition, and they have established a French Jewish presence in French theatre that reflects their reality. Its distinction from the other francophone plays is in its appearance and setting in the *metropole*, France.

IV

Jean-Claude Grumberg has been a successful man of theatre for over forty years, having written more than thirty plays. He is also an actor, a screenwriter (for François Truffaut, *Le Dernier Metro* [*The Last Metro*], 1980; and Costa-Gavras, *Amen*, 2002, and other films), a writer of ten children's plays, a writer of stories and dialogues, and even a stage director. He has won six Molières, the French equivalent of the Pulitzer Prize (two of which are for the full-length plays in this anthology), and a number of other theatrical awards. Many of his plays have their debuts presented by the most prestigious theatre company of France, La Comédie Française, the French National Theatre. *The Workplace* and *Mama's Coming Back, Poor Orphan* were made part of the curriculum for the French baccalaureate degree. In short, his plays have critical acclaim, and his unique vision and style has been appreciated for the last forty years.

Born in 1939 in Paris into a very poor Jewish family of tailors, Jean-Claude Grumberg was too young to understand the early deportation of his Romanian-born father and grandfather as stateless Jews. His mother, a French citizen, managed to get her sons into the Zone libre (the Free Zone) and placed them with a sympathetic farmer. After the war, he returned to Paris and went to a French public vocational school and concluded his certification at the normal age of fourteen to become a tailor's assistant and learned the trade. Along the way he fell into acting and discovered he liked it.

He also discovered that he enjoyed writing plays. His first plays were well received. One of them dealt symbolically with the rise of Nazism (*Amorphe d'Ottenburg*, 1970); another showed how one age prepares disaster for another (*En r'venant de l'Expo* [*Coming Back from the World's Fair*], 1973), using the *café concert* and its songs—a favorite device of Grumberg's dramaturgy—to reveal the frivolity of the Belle Epoque around the World's Fair of 1900, a time caught between militant patriotism and idealist pacifism. Grumberg's humor was early recognized as theatrically effective in revealing the brutal truth beneath the banalities of the age or situation. He was early on considered a serious playwright with a biting wit finding his way to his real voice. He found it creating *Dreyfus*, depicting the European Jewish reality and using his status as a French citizen of Jewish origin. His first three French Jewish plays capture (1) the prewar years (*Dreyfus*, 1974), (2) the war years, 1940–1944 (*Zone libre* [*The Free Zone*], 1990), and (3) the aftermath, 1945–1953 (*L'Atelier* [*The Workplace*], 1979). This last work, his most popular play, established Grumberg as the most important French Jewish dramatist, with the masterful theatrical skill needed to create humanity in his characters and authenticity in their condition, eschewing any effort to create martyrs or saints. His later two French Jewish plays, *Maman revient, pauvre orphelin* [*Mama's Coming Back, Poor Orphan*] (1994) and *Vers toi terre promise: Une tragédie dentaire* [*On the Way to the Promised Land: A Dental Tragedy*] (2009), are memory plays of the French Jewish experience after the war. These French Jewish plays all have strong autobiographical sources and define a French Jewish experience that requires a new appreciation of the expanded concept of French identity that goes beyond Gallic and Frankish roots. Grumberg's plays give voice to a Jewish presence demanding its legitimacy as part of a modern French inheritance. This was inconceivable before World War II, but the French betrayal of the Jews during the war and Occupation created a new Jewish consciousness that is now part of French society and expresses a French Jewish perspective in newly created French Jewish plays.

Both *Mama's Coming Back, Poor Orphan* and *On the Way to the Promised Land* are memory plays that reveal a late development in the dramaturgy of Jean-Claude Grumberg. Whereas *Dreyfus, The Free Zone,* and *The Workplace* present the French Jewish experience in a linear perspective that reflects the mid-century Holocaust and its consequences, the memory plays written at the end of the century and into the new twenty-first century consider the effect of the past, especially the Holocaust experience, on French Jews, including himself, the author, throughout the post-war experience, which extends over more than fifty years. The dramatist seeks to interpret the power of past experiences upon the present and how memory of the past shapes contemporary thinking and action. The passage of the authorial character from outside the earlier plays, as in the first trilogy, into the later plays alters the esthetic space where the authorial character becomes an active participant. This permits a greater dramatic intensity for the audience because the authorial character's role focuses the audience on the events on stage. It brings a stronger identification with the author and permits a greater sense of authenticity of the past events as they affect the French Jewish characters on stage desperately seeking accommodation and resolution to their historical condition.

In the one-act play *Mama's Coming Back, Poor Orphan*, the author is a sixty-five-year-old writer coming out of anesthesia in a recovery room in which time and space are vague and bleed into each another. The author appears to regress to childhood, seeking solace from his isolation as he attempts to recover his mother and father in his mind. He reaches out to them, but they are clutches of memory, uncertainties, freighted with emotion. Memory, providing him with scenes of his youth and his French Jewish childhood in Paris, permits him to conceive of his deported father in terms of historical facts and recalls his childhood projections of a protective father who was removed from his family by the French police. His encounters therefore are both real and fictional but present the power of memory to affect the present.

In the full-length play, *On the Way to the Promised Land*, the playwright's most dramaturgically sophisticated work presented, ironically, as a dental tragedy, Grumberg's character appears from the oblique angle of a child of an afflicted French Jewish family facing the unpleasantness of going to the dentist and facing the drill like a guillotine, the symbol of torture and human misery. The dental chair and drill reflect the ruination of Dr. Spodek's family, who lost their children in the Holocaust. A successful acculturated French Jewish dentist before the war, a wreck afterward, having lost his two daughters, Charles contemplates his misery while his wife, Clara, imagines some restoration of meaning at the terrible price of abandoning La France, this land of liberty, equality, and freedom that had betrayed them. Against the incessant misery of their condition, Grumberg brilliantly depicts with great humor his younger self discovering in the dental chair and ominous drill his first sexual awakenings as the busty Moroccan nurse assistant leans over him, revealing sights of astonishing interest and producing new physiological pleasures unbeknown to him before. A new generation awakens and life will go on! But for the Spodeks, their decision to abandon France underscores the effect of the Holocaust and its consequences. The lack of concern, however, on the part of the young authorial character underlines the comic and pathetic reality that the Talmudic proverb reiterates: a generation comes and a generation goes. A terrible moment of French history and of French Jewish history is encapsulated in this memory play that sets a French Jewish family off to a new Promised Land. The rejection of their homeland has made them stateless even with the restored passport of the Fifth Republic. The play also mocks Grecian dramaturgy, for its heroes have Achilles's heels and are by tradition and necessity of aristocratic origin. Grumberg casts off this Greek vision as useless for modern tragedy. The Spodeks are innocents who become unwilling victims and perform heroically just by seeking to survive and proceed onward. This is the nobility Grumberg admires. This family, with perhaps too much hope, proceeds on its way to a new/

old Promised Land. But Grumberg, at heart a cruel realist, leaves their fate unknown. His authorial character in the play has chosen to live in the French Republic, of which this play's performance asserts the renewed French Jewish presence in France, not just as French citizens but as French Jews.

Grumberg's purely French Jewish works are considered his finest work, but they constitute at most 20 percent of his total output. But Jewish interests can be found in plays as diverse as *Adam et Ève* [Adam and Eve] (1997)—a post-Eden reading—and *H.H.* [Heinrich Heine and Heinrich Himmler] (2011). They are also found in *Rêver peut-être* [To dream perhaps] (1998), a surreal play about the dreams of a French Jewish actor, Gerard—who has been playing Hamlet—that cause him to be hauled before a court of law for murder. It is an attack on state intervention into the private and even oneiric life of a citizen. Even Grumberg's children's plays, which he holds dear, contain clear allusions to Jewish themes, such as the Golom (Golem), the superhuman defender of the underdog in *Mon Étoile* [My star] (2007); or *Le Petit Chaperon Uf* [The Little Red Riding Hood of Uf] (2005), a variant of the Little Red Riding Hood tale, with allusions to the lost father and grandfather, both tailors, deported in 1942 to Auschwitz; or *Iq et Ox* [Iq and Ox] (2003), two friends who flee from warring parents over which God is the real God. Grumberg's skills as a film writer brought him into contact with François Truffaut, and Grumberg supplied him with the dialogue of *The Last Metro* (1980), based on a story of a Jewish director who hid under his theatre's boards during the war. Grumberg also adapted Rolf Hochhuth's play *Der Stellvertreter: Ein christliches Trauerspiel* [*The Deputy, a Christian Tragedy*] (1963) into the scenario for the Costa-Gavras film *Amen* (2002).

Grumberg, unhappy that his character Léon, the boss in *The Workplace*, was, as he thought, misinterpreted, decided to play that role on stage himself to show Léon's complexity, a passive/aggressive *l'homme moyen sensual juif!*, an ordinary man surviving through luck and cunning and desperate to live, inept but not evil. His acting won great appreciation for the depths of his performance. In short, Grumberg represents a consummate man of theatre.

V

Jean-Claude Grumberg experienced the Golden Age of the French Absurd Theatre with its masters, Eugene Ionesco and Samuel Beckett, in the 1950s and 1960s. He observed their art and absorbed their skills. But he rejected their abstractions, language play, and use of circular structure. Grumberg is a theatre man of the 1970s. The post-1968 era sought to deal with quotidian problems and not abstract universals. The new theatre returned to a reworked realism, linear structure with little plotting, if any, and scenes presented as illustrations of the given conditions, influenced by Brechtian epic theatre, and a return to a more individuated characterization, influenced by Eugene O'Neill. The French theatre sought to reach out to a broader mass of people, especially the proletariat throughout France, where national theatres were established to draw in the working-class world. The National Theatre of Strasbourg introduced the Austrian theatre of Franz Xaver Kroetz, whose plays treated the peasant and working classes in Austria trying to accommodate themselves to the modern world and having difficulty articulating their wants and needs. In German, this type of theatre was called Alles Tages Theater and translated into French as Le Théâtre du Quotidien, the Theatre of Daily Life. This new theatre treated mainly the proletariat and not the traditional theatre of the bourgeoisie with its clever plot work and tightly integrated structures from the beginning of the century. The scenes were generally complete in themselves but continued in a chain of references that provide linearity and variants on themes and notes the passing of time. There is also a certain unity of place that projects a physical icon of each play. Dialogues are never the smooth, urbane, and witty balletic performances of traditional French plays; rather, they are interrupted, discontinuous dialogues with gaps and verbal sounds of surprise, pain, or ennui. Grumberg absorbed these new developments and applied them to his treatment of Parisian Jewry, particularly the poor Jews of Eastern Paris in the aftermath of the war.

Grumberg, in his plays, broke with the long tradition of theatrical French elegance performed in a formal vocabulary, diction, and delivery all so witty, orotund, and often empty (best illustrated before the war by the playwrights Jean Giraudoux and Jean Anouilh and in the directing style and performance of the talented Louis Jouvet). Grumberg, himself from the working classes, sought out and captured with precision the shared orality of the contemporary Parisian proletariat and the working-class Jews of the Marais and Ménilmontant of eastern Paris. It is language that gives each character his definition far more than any action or plotting. Grumberg dares to bring the street onto the stage, as Louis-Ferdinand Céline did in his novels before the war. In fact, Grumberg's punctuation before he cast out punctuation entirely—learned from Vinaver's texts—follows Celine's punctuation with his beloved three dots, or *points suspendus*, meaning both an unfinished statement or thought, or a determined pause like a fermata sign in music to give the utterance deeper resonance.

As a pupil of Molière, Grumberg learned not only dialogic structures to produce laughter and reveal character but to use music not only for its dramatic presence but to enrich meaning. Grumberg's use of song, folkloric or street urban melodies, a sudden unexpected musical presence, evokes much of the popular culture of the era and is made integral to the meaning of the work and its evocative power. On a subliminal level the French audience recognizes the melody and is drawn closer to the proceedings on stage: there is fusion of audience and actors. It also reinforces French identity. When music performed is foreign, as is the Yiddish tango in *The Workplace*, it functions on two levels: (1) it establishes the presence of difference between Jews and Gentiles, but (2) it is used as a testing of acceptance as Gentile and Jew join in dance.

Humor and the comic mode are used by Grumberg for shock value and to touch cautiously on evocations of the Shoah. Grumberg also uses sexual humor openly to display the thinking and living reality of people in confined quarters working and working off frustrations. Humor is never innocent in Grumberg's plays; it provides authorial insight for the audience to appreciate the implications of the humor and its objective.

Contrary to those who seek to discover "Yiddish humor" in these plays (and what is Yiddish humor?), the wit and crisp moments of humorous exchange reveal far more the inheritance of French classical comedies, French boulevardier theatre, Voltairian wit, and the broad humor of Rabelaisian risqué joking. The putative "laughter to tears" of Yiddish humor is a Sholem Aleykhem skill, not Grumbergian. Nor does Grumberg use lazzi, or physical humor, to obtain laughter; his humor depends on the turn of the phrase and the situational reality in which something important is at stake. For example:

CLARA: We just received a letter.
CHARLES: Another one?
CLARA: A letter from Gisèle.
CHARLES: Gisèle? What Gisèle?
CLARA: Gisèle of Toulouse.
CHARLES: Gisèle of Toulouse?
CLARA: The one who's in Israel.
CHARLES: Then why are you saying from Toulouse?
CLARA: I'm not talking about Toulouse. I'm talking about my
    cousin Gisèle.
    We call her Gisèle of Toulouse to distinguish her from my
two other cousins with the same name who weren't from Toulouse and who were taken away.

This is Grumbergian humor: humor based on the old Molière tricks of repetition and mistaken identity that stimulate laughter and that Grumberg turns sour. The rug is pulled away and the painful truth emerges.

CHARLES: There's only one Gisèle left?
CLARA: Yes, the one from Toulouse. She lives in Israel.
(*Silence*)

—SCENE II, ON THE WAY TO THE PROMISED LAND

Clara and Charles are French Jews to the tips of their fingers, there is Yiddishkeyt left, the Ashkenazic remains from the pilgrimage to France, their Promised Land as it appeared in Eastern Europe to their parents or grandparents. But they use no Yiddish in any of these French Jewish plays of Grumberg, and only the older generation can understand it. French is their mother tongue. France is home, homeland, and they have to deal with its betrayal. So does Grumberg the artist, and humor serves him well when there is no exit or solution. And as the Gentile audience laughs, suddenly the incongruous occurs, the reality of the Shoah grabs them, too. Humor is important to post-war European Jewish theatre in order to deal with such memories, and Grumberg provides masterly examples of this comic art.

Each play contains, of course, the hidden tragedy that haunts Grumberg's theatre: the broken family. His plays are never about the clashes of personality or debilitating psychological problems tearing a family apart. Rather, his plays reveal what happens when evil strikes and a father or a child is removed by a nefarious political power affecting the individuals of the family and the structure of the family itself. How does a family continue when a member is literally pulled away before one's eyes? How does one go on? Grumberg's plays are about the rescue of the living and urging them to prevail. Remember the lost one but live now fully in one's present, for the past is another country now, and the future never is sure.

The Workplace reveals the coping of various Jews and their putative restoration into the French community across 1945–1953. It proffers a wonderfully intense experience of ordinary proletariat Parisian Gentile workers with their Jewish counterparts. Most critics consider Simone the central figure, for her entrance in the workplace opens the drama and her absence at the end provides a sort of closure. But Léon the boss deserves more scrutiny, for like most of the men in Grumberg's plays, he is not lovable but somewhat *grinçant*, or grating. The same can be said for Charles in *On the Way to the Promised Land* or the Father in *Mama's Coming Back, Poor Orphan*. Life has been hellish for them, but their adaptation and determination to participate in the new reality deserve our appreciation.

But never underestimate the role of the Jewish women and mother figures. They are perhaps more of the life force in Grumberg's dramas than the driven men. They play the classic role of the Jewish wives who appear demure but, like the Jewish women in Egypt in the Passover Haggadah, they prop up their men and move them to live and move on. Grumberg's mother appears in two of the plays as the powerful figure who keeps her emotions in check in front of her men but shows her vulnerabilities to other women. Even in *On the Way to the Promised Land*, Clara is a mother surrogate pushing her husband forward: "Das Ewig-Weibliche zieht uns hinan" (The eternal Feminine drives us onward), as Goethe so well understood. The family, the essential Jewish unit, remains intact despite the losses. The hurt never disappears, but the family will prevail. The memory play *Mama's Coming Back, Poor Orphan* reveals how the ruined family provides the signpost to the present and future, to a satisfactory existence despite the costs.

Grumberg is harsh in his judgment of life, but he associates fully with the concept that living life to one's fullest potential delivers the only answer to the ineffable.

Grumberg's plays are amber capsules of time preserving the drama of a post-Shoah French Jewish generation underlining its will to survive and even participate in Jewish renewal within an indifferent Europe, where their right to be is no less legitimate than any member of the majority culture. Grumberg has created a new dramatic voice for French Jewry to express itself openly in France and in Europe, manifesting its presence through the borrowed esthetic structure of theatre.

Grumberg's plays and vision are hybrid: the fusion of two cultures. Grumberg's identity and expectation is that of the French secular citizen with Jewish roots performing in an enlightened open French universalizing culture protected by the values of the Fifth Republic. Grumberg lets his characters, the Spodeks, leave for their Promised Land, but Grumberg is giving France and Europe one more chance to live up to its ideals of *liberté, égalité, fraternité.*

Jean-Claude Grumberg

A Timeline of Key Works and Life Events

Some of these refugees stay on and lodge
In slums on the rue des Rosiers or the rue des Écouffes
They keep close to home like chessmen
And are mostly Jewish their wives wear wigs
Pallid they sit at the back of little shops

—APOLLINAIRE, ZONE, 1913 (TRANSLATOR UNKNOWN)

1939　Jean-Claude Grumberg is born on July 26 in the tenth Arrondissement of Paris, a working-class district on the Right Bank, to Jewish parents from a family of tailors. His mother was a French citizen born in France, and the father, an immigrant with his parents, had only Romanian papers but served in the French army.

1943　On February 26, Grumberg's father and blind grandfather are deported by the French police to Drancy and shipped to Auschwitz, where they are exterminated. The grandmother, suffering from extreme diarrhea, is left in bed by the French police in her wastes to die, but she survives. Grumberg and his brother are passed into the Zone libre (Free Zone) and live in the countryside with peasants.

1945　Grumberg and his brother rejoin their mother in Paris in their apartment, which they were able to hold on to. He soon attends public school.

1954   Grumberg graduates at fourteen with a *certificat primaire*, the conclusion of his education. He is not tracked into the lycée but instead enters the career of his family as an apprentice tailor. He moves from workplace to workplace and becomes an accomplished tailor. At night, he attends theatre and joins an amateur acting group and eventually becomes a member of a professional troupe and begins writing plays.

1966   On January 12, Grumberg marries Jacqueline Flom.

1968   Grumberg's first full-length play, *Demain, une fenêtre sur rue* [Tomorrow, a window facing the street], performed by a professional troupe, is well received. It deals with World War III, a race war of white "haves" versus the former colonized "have-nots." A cheering French rightist family watches the battles from their fourth-floor window, expecting victory but are themselves destroyed when their building is bombed by their own side. Grumberg is recognized as a serious new playwright.

1970   May 4. Birth of daughter, Olga, who became an actress.

1971   *Amorphe d'Ottenburg.* With this play, Grumberg attempts to deal with the mindset of Nazism, presenting the story as a sort of Grimm's fairy tale, where the brutish hero is an avatar of Ubu Roi, a monster who destroys the people of his father's kingdom while the father protects him. This drama is performed by the Comédie Française actors, establishing Grumberg's credentials as a major contemporary dramatist. He would go on to write over thirty plays in his career.

1974   *Dreyfus.* With this play, Grumberg finds his richest vein of material, treating the Jewish experience in France in itself and as a reflection of the history of modern France. The play portrays threatened Polish Jews performing a play about Captain Alfred Dreyfus's discomfiture in Paris during 1898, as they rehearse amid the violence in Poland in 1933 and the anti-Semitic realities in Germany. *Dreyfus* is the first play ever produced in France that treats the Dreyfus Affair from a Jewish perspective. It opens the possibility for the first time of presenting a distinct French Jewish perspective in French theatre.

1979   *L'Atelier* [*The Workplace*]. Both the author and the critics consider this drama his masterpiece. Written entirely in contemporary colloquial Parisian speech—not formal French theatre speech—*L'Atelier* captures the working-class world of eastern Paris, specialized women garment workers, male pressers, and harassed husband-and-wife owners, laboring basically in a one-room workplace as they produce men's suits before our eyes. The play is in ten scenes, one per year from 1945 to 1952, with 1946 and 1947 having two scenes each. Each scene captures the spirit of the time and reflects the concerns of ordinary French workers, French Jewish workers, and the French Jewish owners as they interact, accommodating to life in post-war France but also revealing the difficult French Jewish readjustment to post-war French life after undergoing the Holocaust and the betrayal of Vichy. Grumberg performs the husband/manufacturer, Léon, with great success in the first production of the drama, making the controversial role empathetic. The play has enormous success and has been performed constantly since throughout France and Europe and even in the United States.

1980   Grumberg collaborates on the scenario for François Truffaut's *Le Dernier Metro* [*The Last Metro*], set in Occupied Paris. He will continue to write scenarios, especially with Costa-Gavras, up to the present. In the 1980s Grumberg also works in theatre as a director and in television adapting plays for television.

1990   *Zone libre* [*The Free Zone*]. This play completes what is considered by the author and critics a trilogy [along with *Dreyfus* and *L'Atelier*] capturing the Jewish experience in mid-century France. *Zone libre* depicts a French Jewish family lodging with a French peasant who protects them as the war swirls around. They adapt to country living, and we see the nobility of the French peasant, representing the best ethical values of the Republic.

1994   *Maman revient pauvre orphelin* [*Mama's Coming Back, Poor Orphan*]. A one-act play, a memory play of the author emerging from surgery and anesthesia, reliving and imagining his childhood while he is isolated in the recovery room. This powerful play of a lost childhood reflects a universal condition and the particular experience of a French Jew trying to make meaning of his past. This play was assigned to all lycée students from 2000 to 2008 as required reading for the exit examination.

1999   With *Le Petit Violon* [The little violin], Grumberg begins writing plays for children's theatre, a genre considered today very important in France. He has produced over ten plays to the present, often in surrealist settings with subtle political and ethical questions intertwined in the plot. There is often a Jewish subtext element in these plays, as in *Le Petit Chaperon Uf* [The Little Red Riding Hood of Uf] (2005), who is stopped by Wolf from wearing her red riding hood and must wear one in yellow because she is an Uf [Juif = Jew].

2002   *Amen.* Grumberg adapts Rolf Hochhuth's German play, *The Deputy*, an indictment of Pope Pius XII for doing nothing to save the Jews, for film. Grumberg writes the French scenario for Costa-Gavras.

2006   *Vers toi terre promise: Une tragédie dentaire* [*On the Way to the Promised Land: A Dental Tragedy*] wins Grumberg his eighth Molière (comparable to the Pulitzer Prize). Mocking the Grecian ideal of tragedy, Grumberg reveals how a French-Jewish dentist's family, ruined by the German Occupation and French complicity and Catholic Church duplicity in refusing to return their one surviving child to them, refuses an unsatisfactory accommodation in post-war France and by an act of will elects to start over in Israel. The Jewish tragic hero must pursue life, no matter how dire, and must resist, persist, and act ethically. In this, Grumberg's most mature play, his savage humor makes bearable for the audience the tragic reality of post-war France and Europe for the survivors.

2008 With *Ça Va?* [How's it going?], Grumberg embarks on a new series of plays made up of short witty dialogues that illustrate human foibles, social hypocrisy, and complicity using the formulaic phrase, *ça va?* Its success leads Grumberg to write *Moi Je Crois Pas*.

2010 Grumberg writes *Moi Je Crois Pas* [I don't believe a word!], where the husband believes nothing and the wife wants to believe everything. Demonstrated through a series of dialogues worked around the phrase *Moi, je crois pas*, the husband can't remember what he doesn't believe, and the wife forgets what she believes. Grumberg also publishes a book of prose, *Pleurnichard* [Crybaby].

2011 Grumberg writes *Si ça va, Bravo!* [If it works, terrific!], a continuation of a series of comic dialogues worked around the title. His favorite actors—the very famous French actors Pierre Arditi and Catherine Hiegel—continue to perform his dialogue plays.

2013 Grumberg writes the scenario *Le Capitale* [Das Kapital], his fourth film with Costa-Gavras, a critique of capitalism. He also writes *Pour En Finir Avec La Question Juive* [To put the Jewish Question to rest], which continues the series of short comic dialogues between the author, an atheist French Jew, and his upstairs neighbor, a typical Parisian with some anti-Semitic tendencies who seeks to probe the mystery of being Jewish. They meet on the staircase, where the author is challenged to explain what a Jew is, what Judaism is, and what the Jewish condition is; why he defends Israel; and how he can be a Jew if he eats pork, doesn't pray, or observe Jewish traditions. Each dialogue ends with an invitation from the neighbor to set a date for the author and his wife to come upstairs for a drink (*un apéro*) that never occurs.

Jean-Claude Grumberg's works have been continually performed in the finest theatres of France—La Comédie Française, L'Odéon, Théâtre du Vieux Colombier, and Théâtre de la Colline. His plays have had some of the best directors in France, including Jacques Fabbri, Jean-Paul Vincent, Maurice Bénichou, among others, and who have worked with Grumberg on more than one play.

THE PLAYS

The Workplace

[L'Atelier]

*The first workplace I encountered in my life was the unused
space in the three-room apartment of my childhood, where
my father had worked before World War II. In the 1950s, my
mother decided to create a bedroom for us. . . . While awaiting
the return of my father, she worked as a finisher in a workplace
that made menswear. Later—when we were no longer waiting
any more, having learned little by little the meaning of the word
"deported"—having become an apprentice tailor, I would get to
know many other workplaces . . .*

*This play is written for my mother, and for all the men and
women whom I saw laugh and cry in the numerous workplaces
in which I worked.*

—JEAN-CLAUDE GRUMBERG

This play opened in Paris on April 18, 1979, at the Odéon Théâtre
de l'Europe.

THE CHARACTERS

(In order of appearance)
HÉLÈNE
SIMONE
GISÈLE

MARIE

MADAME LAURENCE

MIMI

LÉON

THE PRESSER

THE VOICE

THE OPERATORS

SEWING MACHINE OPERATOR

JEAN, THE NEW PRESSER

MAX

THE CHILD

PLACE: IN A PARISIAN WORKPLACE

The workplace is a room in an old building in the east side of Paris in the Marais quarter (the 3rd arrondissement [ward]) or nearby (the 4th and 10th arrondissements). This area once was the aristocratic quarter in the seventeenth and even eighteenth centuries but decayed badly and became a slum area in the nineteenth century, where the poor and immigrants, especially Jews, settled. In these once noble buildings, the rooms were divided and turned into small apartments, and one room usually served as the workplace for making clothing, a major industry in Paris. These workplaces were akin to "sweatshops," with usually one window or two at most and a poorly lit interior, furnished only with necessities of the "needle trade" and with a small number of workers, usually women, usually seated around a large table in an understood hierarchical order. The male workers operated the machines at different tables: the cutter at his table, the presser with his irons at a separate table. The owner and his assistants would be in a side room or at some distance from the worktable where the clothing was made and finished. Each person had a specialty: sewing buttonholes, or putting in linings, and so forth, and they were paid by the piece. (These workplaces still exist in contemporary Paris but now are filled with African and Asian immigrants.)

TIME: JUST AFTER WORLD WAR II

Scene 1, 1945: Making the Cut
Scene 2, 1946: Songs
Scene 3, 1946: Natural Selection
Scene 4, 1947: The Party
Scene 5, 1947: Night
Scene 6, 1948: Competition
Scene 7, 1949: The Death Certificate
Scene 8, 1950: The Meeting
Scene 9, 1951: Building Her New Life
Scene 10, 1952: Max

Scene 1, 1945: Making the Cut

(One morning very early in 1945.[1] Simone, with her back to the audience, sits working at the end of the table. Standing next to another table, Hélène, the wife of the owner, works, too. From time to time she glances at Simone.)

HÉLÈNE: They also took away my sister in '43 . . .

SIMONE: Has she come back?

HÉLÈNE: No. . . . She was twenty-two. *(Silence)* You worked for yourself?

SIMONE: Yes, just my husband and myself. During the busy season we took on a worker. . . . I had to sell the sewing machine last month, he'd hardly be able to start work. . . . I shouldn't have sold it but . . .

HÉLÈNE: You can always find a sewing machine . . .

SIMONE: *(Nodding in agreement)* I shouldn't have sold it. I was offered some coal and . . .

(Silence.)

---

1. Paris was liberated from German occupation at the end of August 1944, but the war continued into May 1945.

HÉLÈNE: You have kids?

SIMONE: Yes, two boys . . .

HÉLÈNE: How old?

SIMONE: Ten and six.

HÉLÈNE: Nicely spaced apart . . . at least that's what people say . . . I don't have children . . .

SIMONE: They get along fine. The older takes care of the younger. They lived in the countryside deep in the Free Zone.[2] When they came back, the older boy had to explain to the younger who I was. The younger one hid behind his bigger brother and didn't want to see me. He called me "Madame" . . .

(She laughs. Gisèle has just entered and stops a moment by the coat rack that serves for both the presser to hang the articles he finished and the women workers to hang their street clothes. She removes her jacket, hangs it up, puts on a smock, and goes to her place. With a nod of her head, she greets Simone and Mme Hélène. The latter does the introductions.)

HÉLÈNE: Madame Gisèle . . . Madame Simone. She's doing the finishing work.

---

2. The Free Zone was established by the Armistice of June 1940. The Germans created two zones: (1) The Occupied Zone in Northern France, which reached to the Loire River and extended to include the long Atlantic coastline down to Spain, and (2) the Free Zone, which extended from the Loire River south to the Mediterranean Sea. This area was headed by Marshal Pétain, who concluded the Armistice with the Germans. Known as the État Français, the Free Zone superceded the Third Republic, which Charles de Gaulle insisted continued in exile. The Free Zone government under Marshal Pétain had Vichy, a spa town, as its capital, and was the name commonly used for this collaborating French government. As the allies reconquered France in 1944, the Vichy government was moved to Sigmaringen, Germany, where those members who did not flee were taken hostage. During the first two years, 1940–1942, Jews fled from the Occupied Zone to the Free Zone and sought refuge in the countryside, often with peasants, and where they earned their keep by working or paying protection money. But Vichy had its own anti-Jewish laws, and Jews were rounded up and shipped to the Occupied Zone for transport to the extermination camps in Poland.

(*Gisèle signals her approval. She and Simone again nod to each other with a little smile. Gisèle gets down to work. Enter Mme Laurence followed quickly behind by Marie. Both greet Mme Hélène with a sonorous voice.*)

MADAME LAURENCE AND MARIE: Bonjour, Madame Hélène.

(*They change into their smocks. Marie finishes buttoning up while already beginning her first piece. Mme Laurence takes her time, even removing her shoes, which she exchanges for woolen slippers. She shuffles to her place on a high stool at the end of the table facing Simone with her back to the window. She thereby dominates the setting. Hélène, while still working, continues the introductions. Simone smiles a little at each new arrival. All four work silently, each at her own rhythm. Hélène, standing in front of her table, bastes the cloths onto the fronts of the jacket. She works quickly, casting an eye on the workers. Enter Mimi. She seems to rush. She is greeted immediately by a verbal sting from Gisèle.*)

GISÈLE: Just fell out of bed again this morning?

(*Mimi, putting on her smock, answers with a hand flick that seems to say, "Don't bother me." Hélène introduces her.*)

HÉLÈNE: Mademoiselle Mimi . . . Madame Simone.

(*Simone smiles at Mimi. Mimi, while sitting down, extends her hand to Simone in a grand gesture. Simone secures her needle in the cloth and shakes Mimi's hand, bothering Marie, who fumes. Mimi casts a sneering look at Marie but does not say a word. As soon as Mimi begins to work, Mme Laurence draws her stool back ever so slightly, saying to her:*)

MADAME LAURENCE: One of these days, you're going to poke my eye out.

(*Mimi lets it pass and works on. Silence. Gisèle hums along unconsciously.*)

HÉLÈNE: Things are going well for you today, Madame Gisèle!

GISÈLE: (*Surprised*) Me? No, why?

HÉLÈNE: Well, I hear you humming . . .

GISÈLE: Me? I don't hum, Madame Hélène. My heart's not in it, especially not these days . . .

(*Her eyes are almost full of tears. Mimi and Marie look at her and burst into laughter.*)

MADAME LAURENCE: (*Casts a long look on Simone's work then remarks*)
You've been doing high-end finishing for quite a while? (*Simone agrees.*) It shows. You make pretty little stitches.

(*Suddenly, M. Léon, the owner, appears for a second at the door leading to the other workplace rooms and harshly shouts out twice:*)

LÉON: Hélène, Hélène!

(*All the women are startled, squeal, and then break out into laughter. Hélène sighs. From the other room Léon is heard, increasingly irritated (perhaps on the phone). Machine sounds are heard. Mme Laurence holds her breast while shaking her head. Simone, who was startled like the others, now laughs heartily. Mimi imitates a dog that growls and barks while Mme Hélène exits, shutting the door behind her. They are heard arguing, then moving away.*)

GISÈLE: We're off to a fine start . . . if they're yelling so early this morning, I . . .

(*She does not finish her sentence.*)

MADAME LAURENCE: There's trouble brewing.

SIMONE: Is it always like that?

MADAME LAURENCE: M. Léon? You haven't met him yet? You'll get your chance.

MIMI: (*In a very hoarse voice, almost voiceless*) It'll happen again.

MADAME LAURENCE: What?

MIMI: It'll happen again.

MADAME LAURENCE: What are you talking about?

MIMI: (*Still speaking hoarsely; she will continue to speak hoarsely to the end of the scene.*) What you said about M. Léon, I'll repeat it to him.

MADAME LAURENCE: (*Taking the others as witness*) That's not fair. She's crazy, this floozy, what did I say? What did I say? (*Mimi scratches her throat without saying a word. Marie stifles a laugh. Mme Laurence stares her down.*) You find that so funny?

MARIE: It's her voice . . . (*She breaks out in laughter. To Mimi*) It's your voice.

MIMI: (*After clearing her throat*) You find it funny? You really don't give a damn about my voice? (*Marie nods in agreement. In the meantime, Gisèle invites Simone to move nearer to the window between herself and Mme Laurence—"for the light." Simone is now facing Mimi. Mimi, now aware of her, continues.*) Some people's bad luck makes fools laugh.

(*Marie, giggling, thanks her.*)

GISÈLE: You've got to laugh, it makes up for no meat.

(*Mimi coughs, Simone searches in her bag and takes out a bottle of cough drops and offers it to her.*)

SIMONE: They're good for the throat . . .

MIMI: (*Taking some*) Thanks . . .

(*Simone offers some to the others who serve themselves.*)

MARIE: (*Reads the label*) "Pectoids, candy cough drops, soothe the cough, sweeten and freshen up the breath."

GISÈLE: (*To Simone*) You can figure out which women have children. (*Simone nods.*) How many?

SIMONE: Two.

GISÈLE: That's work, no?

MIMI: (*Cutting her off*) Why don't you ever pass around candy? You're a mother, too, aren't you?

GISÈLE: I don't even give any to my own kids, you don't expect me to go out and buy some just for you?

MIMI: Why not? I'd like that. . . . You never give anything . . .

(*Gisèle does not respond.*)

MADAME LAURENCE: (*To Mimi*) You'd do best to not say a word. Give your throat a rest for once. (*Mimi sneers and bleats. Mme Laurence pursues.*) It's for your good. If you think of course that you have something important to tell us . . . (*Brief pause. She begins again.*) One free day of peace would not be . . . (*Mimi pushes her stool slightly and most discreetly closer to Mme Laurence's, so close that Mme Laurence is once again bothered by Mimi's arm and threatened by her needle. Mme Laurence stops, pulls back slightly then very politely.*) Might you be so kind—and at little cost—allow me some breathing room?

GISÈLE AND MARIE: (*Together*) My dear . . .

MIMI: What? What did she say? (*Mme Laurence places the piece she just finished next to her, gets up and leaves. Mimi attempts to speak to all around.*) She's raced off earlier than usual, she needs a good plumber to seal her up.

(*But her voice trails off, she attempts to clear her throat and coughs. Simone brings out her bottle. Mimi refuses it with her hand.*)

GISÈLE: (*Dryly to Simone*) You'd do better to keep them for your kids.

MARIE: (*After having tapped Mimi on the back*) Where did you catch that again?

MIMI: (*Raising her shoulders*) I don't know . . . I went dancing last night, I caught it . . .

GISÈLE: Did it rain last night?

MIMI: (*Shakes her head no*) I fell into the gutter. (*Marie breaks out laughing*) Laugh, laugh . . . I was with Huguette, my good old Huguette . . .

GISÈLE: The fat one.

MIMI: She's not so fat . . .

GISÈLE: Huguette. Isn't she the one you call the "fat pig"?

MIMI: (*Agreeing*) That's right. It means she's not really fat, she just appears that way. . . . Both of us were at the dance hall yesterday. I took off my shoes to dance and later I couldn't find them . . .

(*Marie can't stop laughing. Simone begins to giggle a bit too.*)

GISÈLE: You lost your shoes?

MIMI: Someone swiped them from me, yes . . .

GISÈLE: You take off your shoes now to dance?

MIMI: The swing, to dance the swing . . . then two American GIs offered to take us home, and one of them carried me so as not to get my feet dirty, and then I don't remember what they babbled, but at some point he asked me something, and I didn't get a word he said, but I said yes with my head, and my friend said yes, too, then this guy dropped me without any warning right into a puddle in the gutter. I was soaking wet. Huguette with the two GIs broke into wild laughter that turned into a brawl with everyone telling the other off. (*She clears her throat, she's suffering more and more.*) I woke up this morning like this, I couldn't say a word . . .

(*Gisèle, Marie, and Simone double up in laughter.*)

MADAME LAURENCE: (*Returns, takes her usual place, then*) Making fun of me? (*Gisèle, Marie, and Simone shake their heads while laughing even more. Simone tries to stop herself from laughing further as Mme Laurence speaks to her.*) You've caught on quickly I see, well don't worry, I'm used to it. She turns everyone against me.

GISÈLE: (*To Mme Laurence*) We didn't say a word about you, nothing at all . . .

MIMI: (*To Gisèle*) Stop it. . . . It's not nice to lie, especially after what was said. (*She points to Gisèle. Simone has her handkerchief in hand, she is no longer working, she pats her eyes while continuing to excuse herself for each outburst of laughter. Mimi continues.*) There's the proof of what happens when you don't catch their lingo. Huguette told me I should never have nodded yes. (*She pronounces a phrase in "americanese."*)

MARIE: Were they drunk or what?

GISÈLE: So you returned soaking wet and without shoes?

MIMI: (*Who now joins in the laughter*) My skirt stuck to every part of me. . . . It had shrunk, a real dirty trick, this damn piece of junk rayon.

(*They all laugh once again except Mme Laurence, who makes a face. Then little by little order returns.*)

GISÈLE: How can you go dancing like that every night?

MIMI: I go there every night, I was there yesterday . . .

MARIE: (*To Simone*) Are you also going to go dancing?

(*Simone shakes her head, no, while laughing.*)

GISÈLE: She said she has children.

MARIE: It's not forbidden to go dancing when you have children? (*Gisèle shakes her head annoyed.*) You can even go dancing with your husband, right?

SIMONE: (*Simply to stop the topic*) In such times, I'm not going dancing.

GISÈLE: There!

MARIE: And before you used to go there?

SIMONE: From time to time, yes . . .

MARIE: It's your husband who doesn't like to?

SIMONE: (*Taking a pause*) He's not around, he was deported.

(*A short silence.*)

MIMI: (*Pressing on in her hoarse voice*) When I think about that swine, that American . . . Maybe he ran off with my shoes?

GISÈLE: Wonderful! You never should have taken them off. . . . No, I never . . .

MIMI: (*Cutting her off*) Did you go dancing?

GISÈLE: Of course.

MIMI: No kidding!

GISÈLE: When I was still a really young girl.

MIMI: No kidding! You really were young once?

GISÈLE: In any case I never danced with army guys.

MARIE: Why not if they're not Germans.

GISÈLE: It's not as if only Germans didn't do things (*She turns to Simone*) Excuse me, I wanted to say that the Americans at times crossed . . .

(*She stops.*)

MIMI: (*After a moment*) Come on! Spit it out, tell us all . . .

MADAME LAURENCE: What were you really trying to say, Madame Gisèle?

GISÈLE: Nothing, nothing . . .

MADAME LAURENCE: (*Conciliatory*) You'd prefer to have Germans than Americans?

GISÈLE: I didn't say that, don't put words in my mouth . . .

MADAME LAURENCE: (*More and more conciliatory*) Speaking only of good manners of course.

GISÈLE: If you put it that way, well yes, perhaps, although it's all the same, it's like in everything, I mean . . .

MIMI: Do you want to ask them to return, you miss the Germans?

(*She whistles under her breath. Gisèle raises her shoulders. Silence.*)

MADAME LAURENCE: It's just that when the Americans were not around, we prayed they'd come. Now that they're here, we're ready for them to go home.

MIMI: Speak for yourself, they don't bother me, only when they run off with my shoes and plop me in the filthy gutter.

MADAME LAURENCE: I find they lack a little . . .

MARIE: Did one of them show you a lack of respect, Madame Laurence?

(Mimi screams out laughing. Mme Laurence shrugs her shoulders. The door opens. Mme Hélène calls:)

HÉLÈNE: Madame Simone, please. *(Simone rises, puts down the piece, Hélène stands at the door.)* No, no, come with . . .

(Hélène disappears. Simone seems moved.)

GISÈLE: Did you discuss money yet? *(Simone shakes her head no.)* Don't let them get away with anything, you hear . . .

MARIE: *(Whispering as Simone passes her)* Be careful, he's crabby and a bit of a cheapskate.

(Simone exits.)

MADAME LAURENCE: *(To Marie)* What did you say?

MARIE: When?

MADAME LAURENCE: You said something about crab?

MARIE: I said he had fingers like crab pincers.

MADAME LAURENCE: *(After an instant)* I don't understand.

(Marie shrugs her shoulders.)

GISÈLE: He's a decent fellow all the same.

MARIE: *(Annoyed)* That doesn't mean . . .

(Silence.)

MIMI: *(To Marie)* She, too.

MARIE: What?

MIMI: *(Pointing to Simone's stool.)* She, too . . . .

MARIE: She's too, what?

(Mimi makes the gesture of having a big nose.)

MARIE: You're crazy.

MIMI: Oh?

MARIE: I don't believe it . . .

MIMI: I can recognize them, it's easy, I recognize them.

(Marie raises her shoulders.)

GISÈLE: In any case, she's pleasant!

MIMI: Oh la la, that's not saying much. . . . Everyone's quite pleasant with her this morning . . .

GISÈLE: I like her, that's all.

MIMI: Me, too, so there. I like her, too, . . . but that doesn't mean she's not also . . .

MADAME LAURENCE: She has quite the giggle!

(Silence.)

GISÈLE: The poor thing must not have much chance to laugh these days with all the bad news around.

MIMI: So? We all have run-ins in life. Why I've really lost my shoes and I'm not making a . . .

GISÈLE: *(To Marie reproaching her)* And you ask her if her husband likes to dance?

MARIE: Did I know?

MADAME LAURENCE: There are things you can feel . . .

(Marie completes her piece, she clips off its ticket, places it in a box, looks about her. She is angry.)

MARIE: I don't have any more work!

GISÈLE: Go look for some.

MARIE: *(Without getting up)* That's not what I'm supposed to do . . .

GISÈLE: Do you prefer losing a piece rather than moving your ass?

MARIE: If I do it once from then on I'll have to do it again and again. . . . Why don't I have more work?

(Simone has come back, she sits back down in her place.)

GISÈLE: *(Asking her)* So?

SIMONE: It's ok. I think it's ok.

MADAME LAURENCE: Did you work things out with him? *(Simone looks at her without catching on.)* Did you get what you wanted?

SIMONE: Yes, I mean, the usual, I suppose . . .

GISÈLE: You'll see, it'll all work out well, there's work all year round here . . .

MARIE: *(More and more annoyed)* There's work everywhere these days.

GISÈLE: Exactly, one more reason: here, too!

MARIE: What do you think of our boss?

SIMONE: Typical . . . I mean . . . just typical.

MIMI: (*To Simone*) Make bigger stitches now, if you want to move along, they should be a bit longer otherwise . . .

HÉLÈNE: (*Who just entered, to Mimi*) You always give good advice, Mademoiselle Mimi.

MIMI: (*Breaks out laughing*) I didn't hear you enter, Madame Hélène. You should put your wooden heels back on for work, keep your rubber ones for Sunday.

MARIE: Madame Hélène, I finished my piece and . . .

(*Enters Léon, he is very nervous.*)

LÉON: (*To Hélène*) Well, did you tell them?

HÉLÈNE: No, I just arrived . . .

LÉON: What the hell are you waiting for?

HÉLÈNE: (*sighs*) I just came to tell them, I just came to say . . .

GISÈLE: What's going on, Monsieur Léon?

LÉON: She's going to tell you, she's going to tell you . . .

(*He leaves.*)

HÉLÈNE: (*Calling him back*) Since you are already here, tell them yourself.

LÉON: (*From the other room*) If I tell you to tell them, it's not for you to tell me to tell them . . .

HÉLÈNE: (*Addressing the working women while keeping busy putting things in order in the workplace*) We haven't received the cloth they should have delivered to us so Monsieur Léon has not been able to cut. . . . The machinists have gone home. . . . So finish up what you're doing and go home.

MARIE: What? (*Hélène has already left*) What did she say?

GISÈLE: Great. . . . Now how am I to kill this afternoon?

MIMI: You'll go home and find your little hunk of a husband . . .

GISÈLE: If you think that's funny . . .

MARIE: No. But you saw yourself: he didn't receive the cloth, so we're left out in the cold. He doesn't give a damn if we came to work for nothing, did I have to drag myself all across Paris just for "Go home!" It's been planned and that's scary.

MADAME LAURENCE: Well, that's that, ladies.

(She gets up, places her scissors in their box and slides the box into the drawer. Marie and Mimi exit arm in arm. Marie still sounds hoarse. Mimi imitates her laughing. Gisèle and Simone remain seated next to each other. They finish their work in silence.)

Scene 2, 1946: Songs

(A little before noon in 1946. All the workers are on stage. The presser is at his ironing table. Gisèle has a headache, she is taking a pill.)

MIMI: What's bothering you?

GISÈLE: I have a headache.

SIMONE: At least it's not the feet.

(Gisèle can barely swallow the pill. She tries several times.)

MIMI: It's not going down? *(Gisèle shakes her head no and drinks some more water.)* She's got a tight hole in her throat.

(Marie laughs.)

GISÈLE: *(To Marie)* Thanks for your sympathy.

MARIE: What? We can't laugh any more?

GISÈLE: Not all the time.

MARIE: With you it's most of the time.

GISÈLE: I'd like to see how you'd feel.

(She goes back to work.)

MIMI: Don't think about it any more . . .

GISÈLE: How can I not? I told you, my head feels like a ton of bricks.

MIMI: Sing something for us that'll change your mood. *(Everyone insists. Gisèle shakes her head without saying a word.)* You're a pain in the ass.

GISÈLE: I don't feel like singing.

MIMI: Then sing for me, Big Sister.

MADAME LAURENCE: She likes to be waited on.

GISÈLE: Why don't you sing yourself!

MADAME LAURENCE: If I had your gift, it would be . . .

GISÈLE: I get it, ha, sweet-talking me . . .

MIMI: (*Humming*) "I've two big bulls in my stable." Go on! (*She continues*) Two big white bulls . . .

GISÈLE: If I had two big bulls, I'd hardly be hanging around here. . . . (*Pause, then*) The butcher shops are going to shut three days a week . . .

MADAME LAURENCE: Not for everyone: when they're closed in the front, they're open in the back.

MIMI: (*Singing*)

> In the front, in the back
> Sadly as always
> Without fuss or manners
> She's learned to know love.

(*While Mimi sings, Gisèle holds forth.*)

GISÈLE: It's true some people seem to have everything.

MADAME LAURENCE: (*Articulating clearly*) There are such people, but there's not enough for everyone.

GISÈLE: You wonder how they pull it off . . .

MARIE: Can't you talk about something else?

GISÈLE: I'd sure like to see how you do . . .

MARIE: Isn't it the same for me?

GISÈLE: You don't have kids!

MARIE: So? Nor does Madame Laurence . . . nor Mimi . . .

GISÈLE: It's easy when you're young. (*Short silence*) Less bread than in '43!

SIMONE: Their bread is no good . . .

GISÈLE: That's the least of it: they're best in promising fresh new supplies.

SIMONE: It wasn't much better during the war.

GISÈLE: True, but at least it was wartime . . .

(*Silence.*)

MADAME LAURENCE: What can I make this Saturday that would be tasty and fill the gut?

MIMI: Why not horse testicles!

MADAME LAURENCE: C'mon! Really!

MIMI: What's all the fuss: They're tasty and filling . . .

MADAME LAURENCE: My husband invited eight people . . .

MIMI: (*Cutting her off*) Take two pair of horse balls . . .

(*Silence.*)

GISÈLE: It's true you have your husband.

MADAME LAURENCE: What about my husband?

MIMI: Tough work as a cop, right?

MADAME LAURENCE: He has the same rights as everybody else . . .
   the same rights . . .

(*Gisèle is going to say something, pulls back, sighs, and looks back down at her work. Silence. While working, her eyes resting intently on the jacket, Gisèle begins to sing to herself, for herself in an unconscious way. Mimi alerts the others then accompanies her softly but in a grotesque manner. Gisèle stops abruptly. New silence.*)

MIMI: So how's it going, Big Sister?

GISÈLE: You think I don't see when you're making a fool of me?

MIMI: I came in with the second voice to make the song even more lovely.

GISÈLE: Thanks so much.

(*Everyone insists she begin again. Gisèle puts up a determined and silent resistance.*)

MIMI: (*Suggests*) Gisèle darling, we'll all turn around so as not to bother you, even the presser will turn, ok? Our dear presser, won't you turn away? Don't look at the artist, turn your head toward the girls there. . . . (*They all turn about. Mimi follows, turning, her head toward the presser.*) You see, no one is even looking at you, and I won't even do the harmony since you don't like it.

(*Silence. Nothing moves, they have all turned, only Gisèle is in her usual position, she seems absolutely opposed to the idea of singing anything for the foreseeable future. The women continue to work seeking by feel their scissors or their spools on the table to avoid having to face Gisèle. The presser irons, his head hardly turned away. Suddenly, Gisèle starts. She sings a very sentimental song with a strong and sonorous voice. Marie and Mimi hold back their laughter as much as they can. They finally can't stop themselves, pulling in Mme Laurence and Simone as well. But Gisèle has*) *stopped in the middle of a note. She works now in silence with a ferocious drive.*)

MIMI: So why did you stop singing? (*Gisèle does not answer.*) What's up now?

GISÈLE: I'm being made fun of . . .

MIMI: Not at all, we were moved even . . .

GISÈLE: (*Pointing her scissors toward Marie*) She, she was mocking me. . . . (*Marie breaks out laughing.*) Yeah, it's not swing, it's not boogie-woogie . . . (*She hums menacingly*) "There're zoot suit swingers in my neighborhood, Ding-Dong Daddy of the D-Car Line, boom boom, tra la la tsoin, tsoin." (*Speaking*) Now that's great, that's tops.

MARIE: I never said a word to you.

GISÈLE: As soon as I sing she just laughs at me. All you can do is croak your jangling junk tunes instead of letting others sing, it's easy to mock.

(*She imitates again a zoot suit swing song in a nasal twang.*)

MARIE: What's bugging her?

MIMI: What's up, Gisèle darling, what's bothering you? You look as if you ate crow?

GISÈLE: Everything's going to hell here, you don't give a damn about anything now. All I hear are your shrieks straight out of the jungle, you bounce about in all directions, respecting nothing, no pride in your work.

(*Mimi whistles the song that Gisèle interrupted.*)

MARIE: (*To Gisèle*) What are you saying?

GISÈLE: The young ones here don't even know how to sew, that's what I'm saying, and I'm not the only person to say it, either, believe me . . .

MARIE: (*Rising from her seat*) Enough! Will you! Stop it!

GISÈLE: No! Shithead. . . . Wasn't it you who . . .

(*Marie gets up fully, lets her work fall, seizes the edge of the table that she lifts slightly, everything slides away.*)

MARIE: (*Screaming*) Shut up, do you hear, Shut up!

(Gisèle rises up. Mimi, Simone, and Laurence continue to sew while trying to hold on to their spools, which roll about on the table. The presser has put down his iron, he makes a move to them and starts to joke.)

THE PRESSER: Go on, fight, kill, but don't hurt yourselves.

MARIE: Who asked you to butt in?

(The presser retreats. The operators put their heads in as they pass the door to find out what's going on. Gisèle yields first: she drops her work and exits running, bumping into the sewing machine operators. Marie lets go of the table and falls back onto her stool. The operators demand:)

THE OPERATORS: What the hell's going on here?

MIMI: *(Screaming at them)* Why don't you get lost? Nothing's going on, nothing, we don't need any knuckleheads here. We don't come and bug you in your cubbyholes, right? So shove off. . . . *(The operators draw back. Marie suddenly collapses in tears on the table, she pulls herself together quickly and picks up her work.)* It's a joke how one person weeps in the shithouse and another weeps here. Shit! *(Mme Laurence disapproves shaking her head and hisses through her teeth.)* Stop it, that drives me nuts.

(Mme Laurence keeps on hissing without stopping. Silence.)

SIMONE: There are days where nothing works, even the thread breaks all the time . . .

(Mimi finishes her piece. She doesn't start with a new one. She looks through her shopping bag and pulls out her metal lunch box and finishes.)

MIMI: This is not enough to cut my appetite. . . . But it's nice and warm, so Parisian, no?

(She passes her metal lunch box to the presser, who removes his iron from the gas heater and places the metal food container in its place.)

THE PRESSER: Are there any others?

(Mme Laurence brings her own. Marie lets go of her piece, gets up, and exits grumbling.)

MARIE: I'm grabbing a bite downstairs.

(Once she's gone, Mme Laurence, Simone, and Mimi make faces regarding Marie's departure.)

MIMI: *(Finishing)* Well, what do you know . . .

MADAME LAURENCE: (*To Simone*) You've never brought anything to warm?

SIMONE: I don't have time to prepare anything.

MADAME LAURENCE: You haven't had the strength to . . .

MIMI: You've got to eat crap . . . otherwise . . .

MADAME LAURENCE: You've got to eat some fatty foods! (*Mimi and Mme Laurence set up a semblance of a place setting at their corner of the table; while waiting for their bowls to heat they go back to work. Simone has also finished her piece, takes out a little food bag from her purse and begins to nibble. Mme Laurence to Simone*) You must taste my . . .

MIMI: Is it a day with or without, Madame Laurence?

MADAME LAURENCE: Even when it is without, I make it appear as if it's with.

MIMI: How do you like that?

MADAME LAURENCE: (*Explains while giving Simone something to taste*) When I make a stew, even if I don't have a piece of meat, I always put in some bits of sage, like that, then, after it floats up, it's the taste of leg of lamb that rises up . . .

MIMI: And when you fart?

MADAME LAURENCE: (*Affected*) I do beg your pardon but we are at a dining table . . .

(*Gisèle comes back. And finding Marie's stool unoccupied . . .*)

GISÈLE: Well, well, there's one who refuses herself nothing . . .

MIMI: Oh . . .

(*She signals Gisèle to hold her tongue. Gisèle shrugs. She takes out her own metal food container and brings it over to the presser.*)

THE PRESSER: I have to warm up two more then?

(*Gisèle doesn't answer. She fills an empty bottle at the faucet behind the pressing table and brings it to the worktable.*)

GISÈLE: We ought to pool our money and buy some lithine and that way we could have hot water all the time . . .

MIMI: So buy it, buy it if you have the cash to throw around . . .

GISÈLE: I don't believe in being stingy when it's a question of health.

(*They are now all seated and eating. In the courtyard a voice can be heard. A man is singing "Les Roses Blanches."*[3] *They listen, eating. Mme Laurence has opened the window. Simone, who finished first, gets up and sits by the window. She leans out to see better. Mimi and Gisèle are astir.*)

MIMI: Have they given him any coins?

MADAME LAURENCE: No. Ah, the poor guy . . .

MIMI: Let's give him twenty coins and buttons, that would make more of a jingle . . . .

(*Simone is joined by Gisèle, then by Mimi, who throws down the little bag of coins and some buttons wrapped in a piece of newspaper. The voice interrupts his singing to call out:*)

THE VOICE: Thank you, Ladies and Gentlemen.

(*Simone returns to her place and starts a new piece. Mimi takes another five minutes for herself after the meal. She smokes a cigarette while observing the others who are working. She stares, surprised at seeing Simone weeping quietly.*)

Scene 3, 1946: Natural Selection

(*A late afternoon in 1946. All the women workers are on stage. No one is at the pressing table.*)

SIMONE: Some guy followed me yesterday.

MIMI: Oh yeah? And with the face you make when you walk alone . . .

GISÈLE: Let her speak.

---

3. "White Roses." In Paris and throughout European cities for at least three centuries or more, itinerant singers have entered the courtyards of both poor and middle-class apartment buildings generally in the warm months and sung either traditional songs and ballads or some new popular song of the hour. "White Roses" is a typical sentimental ballad of a poor boy with only his mother, to whom he gives a few white roses every Sunday that he has bought only for her. Alas, one Sunday he returns from buying white roses and finds her gone. She has died from overwork and illness. He promises she will have white roses forever in heaven.

MIMI: I ran into her the other day, and was frightened sick, I swear, she's a busy mouse trotting along fast, one two one two.

SIMONE: It was yesterday, I was coming out of the Red Cross, I had to leave them a photo . . .

MARIE: Of yourself?

SIMONE: No, of my husband. I was annoyed because I hardly had any strength left to drop it off. . . . In any case . . . as usual, I raced along, not really looking ahead, I get on the line, then it's my turn, and boom, I'm outside and bump right into this guy.

MARIE: What did he look like?

SIMONE: A blah type of guy. . . . I say, Excuse me, and he says, Excuse me, we both spout something and who knows I must have smiled at him unconsciously.

GISÈLE: Oh my! Never smile. Never . . . better to insult!

SIMONE: Well I did smile, that's that, I was dead tired, I couldn't even get myself away and everything was bla bla bla and bla bla bla.

MARIE: What was he saying to you?

SIMONE: Do I know? I wasn't listening.

MADAME LAURENCE: Was he vulgar?

SIMONE: Not really. He spoke of my eyes . . . nonsense . . . all nonsense, I didn't dare leave the subway car.

MARIE: Was it in the street or in the subway?

SIMONE: I had to take the subway to get back home.

GISÈLE: He followed you into the subway?

MADAME LAURENCE: There always are types who have nothing else to do.

SIMONE: That's just what I said to him: Don't you have anything better to do?

GISÈLE: You spoke to him? Ay ay ay, Never speak . . .

SIMONE: I finally became afraid. . . . I didn't dare get off at my stop.

MARIE: Were there a lot of people at the subway stop?

SIMONE: Not too many, happily. I mean . . .

MIMI: What could he do to you? A kid hanging on your back under your cloak?

SIMONE: You're a real gift from God! . . . I should have liked to see you in my place . . .

GISÈLE: No danger of that, she's the one who grabs them in the train and they scram to avoid being accused as the deadbeat father of the child.

MARIE: You can also meet nice people at a dance. But it's not really so, it's in the bus . . . because I have to take the same one every day. So, what happened in the end?

SIMONE: I told a cop that some guy was after me . . .

MIMI: And the cop scared you shitless?

MADAME LAURENCE: They're not all the same!

MIMI: Sorry, don't tell me, I get the heebie jeebies with a cop, but never with a guy who speaks of my eyes!

MADAME LAURENCE: Cops are not like that, they serve the public . . .

MIMI: Just go tell him that, ha!

GISÈLE: As in everything there's the good and the bad . . .

(While Mimi smirks . . .)

MIMI: Yeah yeah yeah . . .

(Mme Laurence supports Gisèle.)

MADAME LAURENCE: Exactly!

SIMONE: Those who came in '42 were the more accommodating sort: there was one who insisted on carrying my bundles straight to the commissariat.

GISÈLE: They arrested you?

SIMONE: It wasn't me they wanted, it was my husband. But since he wasn't around, they took me and the kids instead, to the commissariat right next to the 10th Precinct headquarters. . . . There the commissioner, very kind, too, looked at my papers and told me to go back home, that they were not arresting Frenchmen, they did not have any order for that . . .

MADAME LAURENCE: Your husband wasn't French?

(Simone shakes her head, no.)

MIMI: Holy smokes, you must have been frightened out of your wits, poor thing.

SIMONE: I quickly gathered up my bundle,, the two kids and . . . only the older one didn't want to leave like that, he wasn't happy: "Can't anyone carry my mother's package?" He cried out: "You made us come here for nothing." I yanked him by the arm, I thought I had pulled it out of his socket, we left, running all the way home . . .

(*She laughs, everyone laughs.*)

GISÈLE: (*Wiping her eyes*) Poor thing . . .

SIMONE: At home only one thing was missing; a big pocket watch that my husband had received from his father that was always left on the kitchen sideboard.

MIMI: It was one of those hobnailed boots that swiped it.

SIMONE: That surprised me because they tended to be willing to help and all. . . . Not like those who came after and took my husband: they knocked down the door with their feet.

MARIE: Why did they do that?

SIMONE: They knocked, we didn't open, then . . . the owner said it was up to me to have the door repaired. . . . I've already had it done but you can still see the traces naturally, it's not like a brand-new door. . . . Apparently it still shocks those passing the stairway. Might be better to redo the paint, too, yeah, it's peeling and flaking off all over . . . well . . .

(*Silence.*)

MARIE: And this guy?

SIMONE: Which guy?

MARIE: The guy, what was he like?

SIMONE: (*Evasively*) A guy . . .

MARIE: Young?

SIMONE: Ordinary . . .

MADAME LAURENCE: You should have told him that you had kids and were in a rush, there's always a way to show them . . .

SIMONE: I did just that: I told him I had two big children, "I love children," he answered me!

GISÈLE: Shit!

MADAME LAURENCE: Everything depends on the tone.

SIMONE: What does that mean?

MADAME LAURENCE: (*Repeats*) Everything depends on the tone.

(*Short silence.*)

SIMONE: I did nothing wrong you know . . .

MIMI: Don't listen to her, she's an old grouch..

MADAME LAURENCE: Odd that this never happens to me! (*Mimi breaks out in laughter*) Laugh, laugh all you want, they know who they're dealing with.

SIMONE: I made it clear he was wasting his time. What else could I do?

MADAME LAURENCE: No one is accusing you of anything.

SIMONE: She's getting on my nerves.

GISÈLE: You should never answer them—insult them, insult them!

(*Silence. They work now with intense energy, hurrying to finish the pieces so that they can leave. Night is falling. One by one after having finished, they line up their pieces, order their work, some count their tickets then change clothes and depart. Enter Hélène. She sits down in front of her basting table and begins to work while the women workers exit. On the pressing table a pile of clothing lies unironed. When the last worker exits, Hélène stops for a moment from basting her fabrics and begins to put them in order. She's evidently quite displeased. She sorts the buttons that are all mixed up, arranges the spools, folds the unfinished jackets, and hooks together certain clothes that are slipping from hangers. Léon enters. He takes a quick look at the pressing table.*)

LÉON: He never came to work?

HÉLÈNE: Who?

(*Léon points to the pressing table. Hélène shrugs her shoulders.*)

LÉON: We must tell him to appear at regular hours, either the morning or the afternoon . . . he must know that we count on him . . .

HÉLÈNE: Tell him yourself.

(*She sits down again in front of her basting table.*)

LÉON: Why? Why me? (*Silence*) What does that mean: tell him yourself? (*Silence*)

HÉLÈNE: (*While working*) If you've got things to tell him you can tell him, it's as simple as that.

LÉON: He doesn't iron well. He works poorly, I should never have taken him on. (*Silence*)

HÉLÈNE: (*With difficulty*) I cannot stand looking at him . . .

LÉON: Don't look at him . . . Speak without looking . . . (*A moment*) Alright, fine, . . . I'll tell him, I'll tell him . . . (*He starts to leave and turns back on his heels and continues.*) It's terrible, especially since he was deported he shouldn't work, what does that mean? "I can't look at him," what does that mean? He's a man like any other, yes or no? (*Hélène doesn't answer.*) What's wrong with him, what's wrong with him? He's as strong as an ox, all day he holds an iron weighing five kilos in his hands, when he doesn't iron here, he works the small press at Weill's place,[4] and I am sure he has a third job in the evening and a fourth for the night shift. . . . The only thing I want him to do is tell me when he's at Weill's place and when he's here. That's all . . . that's all. I want only workers like him, that's all I can wish for, made of iron, of iron, never a word, never a thought, he knows what it is to work. Don't worry, don't let it bother you, those who've come back from there, they know . . . that's what natural selection is all about . . . (*Hélène says nothing. She stops working, she leaves brusquely, wiping her eyes. Léon follows her.*) That's the truth, that's it, go discuss something seriously with her . . . (*He exits, putting out the lights.*)

Scene 4, 1947: The Party

(*The end of the afternoon, everyone is working. Marie and Gisèle, after looking at the clock, get up and start preparing for the party.*)

GISÈLE: (*To those who are still working*) Come on, time to stop working. (*Then pushing the table against the wall*) Drop your work, we've got to set things up.

MIMI: Let me finish my piece!

SIMONE: (*Getting up*) You'll finish it tomorrow.

---

4. Weill was an important and large manufacturer of menswear in Paris after the war.

MIMI: (*Continuing to work intensively*) She'll talk to any so-and-so in the public bus, and I have to give up a piece?

MARIE: (*Grabs the piece from the hands of Mimi, laughing*) Come on. Stop!

MIMI: Why are they driving me up the wall? Am I suddenly getting married?

(*At the same time, Mme Laurence gets up, removes her smock, and puts on her coat.*)

MARIE: (*While putting on her makeup*) What are you up to, Madame Laurence?

MADAME LAURENCE: I'm going home, darling.

MARIE: You're not staying for . . .

MADAME LAURENCE: Unfortunately, I don't choose the people I work with, but when it's time for having fun, I prefer . . .

MIMI: A question of having fun, well she sure doesn't get much chance to choose.

GISÈLE: (*Who passes a comb once through her hair*) Come, come, Madame Laurence, everyone likes you here.

MADAME LAURENCE: Pure nonsense: I know what I know.

MARIE: Stay for me, it would give me so much pleasure.

MADAME LAURENCE: I wish you a very good time, my dear, and to all of you, but I've finished my work and I have a train to catch.

MIMI: (*Preparing herself, too*) Let her be, if Madame is too proud to drink with us.

SIMONE: (*After having put on makeup also*) Madame Laurence, if we don't make use of these occasions to make peace!

GISÈLE: Of course, this isn't the day to open one's mouth!

MADAME LAURENCE: As long as there are those talking behind my back!

(*She stops a moment by the door.*)

GISÈLE, SIMONE, AND MARIE: What's there to think! Come on. She gets on her high horse, it's ridiculous.

MIMI: (*To Mme Laurence*) Did you mean those words for me?

SIMONE: Don't be silly, she wasn't speaking about you.

MIMI: Did you mean those words for me?

MADAME LAURENCE: If the shoe fits . . .

MIMI: It's out of good manners that I prefer to speak behind your back, think about that!

MADAME LAURENCE: No, you think about that! I don't like that, and since we didn't grow up in the same place, I would ask you . . .

MIMI: (*Cutting her off*) Whether the same place or not . . .

GISÈLE: C'mon, time to make up, shake hands, and let's not talk about it anymore.

MIMI: Me? Shake her hand! Never! Look here, you clearly didn't look, I'm an honest woman, I am!

MADAME LAURENCE: That came pouring out of her mouth fast!

MIMI: Ok! So now it's out in the open. You want to know what I really think of you behind your back?

MADAME LAURENCE: I couldn't give a damn, put that in your pea brain, good evening!

MIMI: (*Stopping her from leaving*) Oh no, no, no! That would be much too easy, she spreads her shit around, she fucks up our party, and she thinks she'll walk off holding her head high.

(*She pushes her into the center of the workplace.*)

MADAME LAURENCE: (*Pulling back hysterical*) Don't you dare touch me!

SIMONE: Mimi! Madame Laurence!

MIMI: Do you really want to know what we think of you? We're sick and tired of your airs, sick and tired, you hear? And here's one thing more to stick inside that thick skull of yours, you weren't born with that stool up your ass!

MADAME LAURENCE: What in the world has she said? What in the world? Get me out of here . . .

MIMI: (*Pursuing*) While we burn our eyes out all year long under the electric lights, Madame sits by the window as if by divine right! No! This . . .

MADAME LAURENCE: That's my place, I have absolutely no reason to change places, I'll never change places.

MIMI: Tomorrow, it'll be my very own buttocks that will be seated there! I, too, have the right to act as the all-seeing watchdog from time to time, right?

MADAME LAURENCE: What?

(Léon enters panic-stricken. Hélène follows him, dressed and made up.)

LÉON: What's going on here again?

MADAME LAURENCE: Monsieur Léon, Monsieur Léon, it's starting all over again.

LÉON: What's starting all over again?

MADAME LAURENCE: *(Pointing out Mimi)* She wants to take my place.

MIMI: Why is she glued to the window, why can't we take turns?

GISÈLE: One week one, one week another, that would be more fair, wouldn't it?

MADAME LAURENCE: You see, you see, they're all in it together.

LÉON: What's all the fuss to be by the window or not? The place is full of fresh flowing air, isn't that so?

MIMI: For that reason alone we're afraid she'll fall sick.

GISÈLE: We want to breathe a bit, too.

MIMI: We can't see anything, Monsieur Léon, in your fucked-up workplace. Our eyes burn in their sockets, do you get what we're saying? And why should Madame monopolize that window with all its sunlight?

LÉON: Whose talking of sunlight, there's never any sunlight, in five minutes time, it'll be pouring . . .

MIMI: To get the window opened, we have to beg her. Madame gets cold easily, and when we want to close it, Madame's having her monthly and a spell of dizziness. It's a pile of shit!

GISÈLE: And besides, she takes advantage of her position to look outside and refuses to tell us what she sees. Well, too bad, I've said my piece, I'm sorry but . . .

LÉON: *(Opening the window and looking out)* There's nothing to see, nothing to see, only the courtyard, the courtyard, there's absolutely nothing to see.

MIMI: Exactly, we just want to see for ourselves.

LÉON: Ok, ok, I got the message, you tell me there's a party, we stop early because Marie is getting married, I agree, why not! I'm not a swine, we're civilized, But you're turning this into a revolution! And if that's so, the party's over, sit down and get to work!

MIMI: (*Cutting him off, shouting even louder*) We want better lighting, we don't want to burn our eyes out, and we've had enough of favoritism here, it's got to go, and we're sick and tired of your rotten stools, we want real chairs—so there!

MADAME LAURENCE: (*Low to Léon*) Monsieur Léon, they hold it against me because my husband's in government service. That's the truth, tell them, these jealous women.

GISÈLE: Yes, Monsieur Léon, chairs!

SIMONE: But who's saying a word about your husband, Madame Laurence, who?

MADAME LAURENCE: Yes, my husband is an official, and I'm perfectly proud of that!

MIMI: (*Singing*) Maréchal nous voilà, / C'est le sauveur de la France.[5]

MADAME LAURENCE: (*Charging toward her with tight fists ready to fight*) And so what, so what!

(*Short silence. Mimi turns her back on her and stifles breaking out in laughter.*)

LÉON: All right, is this over now? Is it over?

MIMI: (*To Gisèle*) There's more than meets the eye!

MADAME LAURENCE: You said plenty more than what you'd ever dare repeat.

MIMI: Try it! I dare you!

LÉON: That's enough now, more than enough!

MARIE: (*On the border of tears*) You're both cruel, the one time I'm getting married.

LÉON: Well said. That'll teach you to make threats and put on airs. . . . The end result is we've lost a good hour and all in tears . . .

---

5. "At your service, Marshal Pétain, the savior of France": Mimi sings words from the hymn "Maréchal, nous voilà," which was sung as a public loyalty oath during World War II to the chief of state of the Vichy government, Marshal Pétain. Mimi's intention here is to brand Madame Laurence and her husband as collaborators.

(Mme Laurence is drawn off by Hélène and Simone.)

HÉLÈNE: Stay, give her a little pleasure.

MADAME LAURENCE: No, no, and no! And after they've insulted me . . . *(She makes a gesture of indifference)* but that they insult my husband, never!

SIMONE: No one's said a word about your husband, Madame Laurence, we've never seen him.

MADAME LAURENCE: That's all we'd need! *(In a low voice to Hélène)* He saved Jews, you know.

HÉLÈNE: Of course, of course.

MADAME LAURENCE: And not like others, for cash, no, never!

SIMONE: Really, take your coat off! Otherwise you'll catch cold outside.

(Mme Laurence lets them remove her coat and whispers:)

MADAME LAURENCE: He even went and warned them before.

HÉLÈNE: Who still thinks about all that, Madame Laurence, who still thinks about all that . . .

MADAME LAURENCE: He took risks . . .

LÉON: What are Hélène and the operators doing?

MIMI: Oh no! Not those guys, this party's closed to them.

LÉON: And what about me?

MIMI: You're not a man, you're a boss. We know what you want!

LÉON: Ha-ha, and the presser, he's not a man either?

(The presser makes a gesture excusing himself for being present.)

MIMI: A harem always needs its eunuch . . .

(Enter the operators.)

THE OPERATORS: Is this the place to get drunk? Whose show is it?

LÉON: Marie is getting married, so . . .

HÉLÈNE: The little presser girl left, we forgot to tell her . . .

(The Operators move more center stage and press around Marie.)

THE OPERATORS: The only one worth sleeping with . . . let's roast her a bit . . . so where's your gigolo, ha?

(While Gisèle and Marie pull out wine bottles, Simone goes and retrieves the gift. Then, waiting for the appropriate silent moment:)

SIMONE: On behalf of all my comrades . . .

(Marie breaks out in sobs and hugs Simone.)

MARIE: You shouldn't have, you shouldn't have.

SIMONE: *(Sobbing, too, while hugging Marie tightly, repeating)* May you only know happiness!

MIMI: That's done, we're off to a good start, on to the drinks, music, damn it, music!

(She sings. Everyone, male and female, hugs Marie, who is crying in front of the unwrapped gift.)

MADAME LAURENCE: I, too, contributed for the gift, my dear, with all my best wishes.

MARIE: *(Hugs her tightly)* Thank you, thank you.

(Léon returns running, carrying a record player and some records. He puts a 78 rpm disc on the record player. It's a tango sung in Yiddish.)

MIMI: What is that?

LÉON: A tango. You don't know what a tango is?

SIMONE: *(Explaining to Marie and Gisèle)* No, it's not German, it's Yiddish.

(She translates the off-color words of the tango with laughter and gusto.)

GISÈLE: What is Yiddish?

SIMONE: What the Jews speak.

GISÈLE: And you can speak it, too?

SIMONE: Yes.

GISÈLE: Then you're Jewish?

SIMONE: Of course.

GISÈLE: Of course, I must be dumb, it's so . . . how funny.

SIMONE: What's so funny?

GISÈLE: Nothing. I knew that Monsieur Léon was, his wife as well, but you . . . I can't get over it. . . . It's, it's odd, don't you think, yet it's so . . . in fact maybe you could tell me then what was really going on between you and the Germans during the war? *(Simone listens without saying a word. Gisèle continues)* I mean, how do you explain that you the Jews and they the Germans . . . it just seems . . . excuse me, I don't know how to put it? There just seem to be many points of agreement, aren't there? I was speaking with my brother-in-law the other day, and he told me:

Jews and Germans before the war were, to put it simply, pretty tight. . . .

(*Simone does not reply, she looks at Gisèle.*)

LÉON: (*Dancing with Marie, and pushing the presser toward Simone*)
Do you know how to dance?

THE PRESSER: Me?

LÉON: (*Throwing him into the arms of Simone*) Then invite her, invite her, she has only two kids and an apartment with three rooms.

(*The two couples circle, everyone is having a good time and drinking. Mme Laurence is seated in a corner, in her coat, her purse on her knees, she has a wine glass in her hand. Léon murmurs some off-color language into the ear of Marie that makes her turn red and laugh. Mimi is now dancing away with a tiny little operator who chats her up in Polish. She makes little winks to Simone and shows her how to "make out." Léon hastens to turn the disc.*)

HÉLÈNE: (*Near the machine*) Don't you have something else?

LÉON: What?

HÉLÈNE: I don't know. Something more ordinary.

LÉON: I don't catch what you're saying.

HÉLÈNE: Oh come on, it leaves a bad taste.

LÉON: What? (*Hélène shrugs her shoulders. Léon holds himself in.*) Who's finding it leaves a bad taste? (*Hélène shrugs her shoulders and goes away. Léon follows her while the new tune begins. It's a waltz in Yiddish.*) Who's finding it leaves a bad taste?

HÉLÈNE: I said nothing. I said nothing. It's just fine. Ok?

LÉON: If you have something to say, say it.

GISÈLE: (*Hugging Marie*) I gotta go home, it'll soon be your turn: ten minutes late and you'll find bedlam.

MADAME LAURENCE: (*Gets up, a bit high*) I'll go down with you. . . . You've got to train him, got to train him, otherwise . . .

SIMONE: (*To the presser*) Do you want to?

THE PRESSER: Let's dance away!

SIMONE: It's a waltz.

THE PRESSER: I don't know if . . .

SIMONE: One has to swirl, that's all.

THE PRESSER: Do you like that?

SIMONE: To dance?

THE PRESSER: No, the Yiddish?

MIMI: (*Dancing still in the arms of the operator*) Take a look at the young couple there, are things starting to bubble?

THE PRESSER: (*He embraces Simone.*) Shall we dance?

SIMONE: Let's!

(*The presser takes the plunge, both of them just miss falling down together. Simone breaks out laughing while the presser excuses himself. In a corner, Léon and Hélène are arguing.*)

Scene 5, 1947: Night

(*The Workplace is in semi-darkness. Simone is working away silently. In front of her, candles or an oil lamp. The presser, sitting on his pressing table, is waiting with nothing to do.*)

SIMONE: I have more than enough for a long time . . .

THE PRESSER: (*Groaning*) No one is waiting for me . . . (*Silence*)

SIMONE: They're still not giving any official death certificate, some lady told me they had told her that the "missing in action" designation was enough. That depends, however . . . To obtain a pension, it's not enough. . . . They make us fill out new forms, we hardly know what rights we have. . . . No one knows anything. . . . They ship us from one office to the next. (*Pause*) Forced to stand in lines everywhere, we end up knowing each other, talking and telling each other our stories. . . . Oh, the cock-and-bull stories that make the rounds. . . . And then there are those who are always in the know. . . . The worst are the mothers. . . . You also came through Hotel Lutetia?[6] (*The presser*

---

6. Hotel Lutetia was and is the grandest hotel on the Left Bank in Paris. During World War II it was taken over by the Gestapo, and horrors occurred there. When the war ended, Hotel Lutetia became the entry point for the deported survivors back from the concentration camps. The hotel redeemed itself, as it were, by becoming the welcoming point back to France. Some survivors stayed at the hotel, but most moved on. It was at this hotel that announcements

nods in agreement.) They told me to go there at the very beginning to get any information, someone who might have seen
him, who . . . you know: the photos, the . . . I only went there
once, I was afraid to go in. Some good woman grabbed my
arm and pulled me to a type of school graduation photo, I see
the kid, he was the same age as my oldest one in short pants,
with a tie, a book in his hand. "First prize," she screamed: "He
always won first prize." She wouldn't let me go, Why are you
crying? she repeated, Why are you crying? Look, look. They're
coming back, they'll all return, God wants it! God wants it!
Then another woman shouted louder than her and began to
push her. . . . It was no use telling them that there was no hope
for the children. There they are, the women, they come and
talk their hearts out, . . . I saw her many times in the various offices, more and more crazed, . . . I spotted another, who never
would stand in a line, Madame expects to be served first, I told
her once: "You know, Madame, we're all in the same boat, no
use trying to wrangle, there's more than enough misery to go
around for everyone." At the Precinct Offices, I met a Madame
Levit with a *t*, she was very kind, a well-off lady, she really had
bad luck, her husband had been taken in '43, but he wasn't
even Jewish, you hear! He had the name Levit, that's all. . . .
And now she never stops running: at the beginning of the war
it was to prove that he was . . .

(She searches for the exact word.)

THE PRESSER: *(Prompting)* Innocent?

(Simone agrees.)

SIMONE: And now like us she runs about only to find out what's become of him and to attempt to obtain a little something: a single mother with three children, without a skill, she doesn't
know how to make anything. . . . *(Silence. The presser looks at her*

---

were posted about the deported, their return, and those not yet returned. Rela-
tives, husbands, and wives would come by, desperate to find out if a loved one
were still alive and returning. Advice was given, but nothing was certain or totally stated. People spent days at the hotel waiting and sharing their tales of woe.

without saying a word. Simone picks up from where she left off.) Yes,
the hardest part is not to know, they think that maybe he's lost
somewhere, not knowing his name anymore, not remember-
ing me or the kids, it happens, it happens, but I tell myself,
that time will heal. . . . The other day I was leaving the mar-
ketplace, and I saw a man from behind with a shopping bag
in his hand, I don't know why, I said to myself, for just a second, I thought: It's him! . . . with a shopping bag! It's funny because he didn't even want to go buy a loaf of bread, he never
ran an errand, he didn't like to . . . Well, it simply means we
think at times of . . . (*A pause*) And so, even if the Precinct Office doesn't want to give a death certificate, it's because they
still have some hope. That even they are certain of nothing,
but they'd be most happy to process the papers and arrange all
the dossiers so that everyone is taken care of and no one would
talk about it anymore. There, I've finished.

(*She gives him the piece. The presser lights his lamp on the table and begins to iron.*)

THE PRESSER: (*While ironing*) Recently they laid claim to my pre-war
paycheck receipts, I said that as I was shipped off with them,
I returned without them. . . . After giving me a nasty look, the
lady told me to have duplicates made. . . . How could I make
duplicates when there aren't any originals? She then advised
me to go see my former bosses and to ask them for copies. I
thanked the lady and left. . . . I didn't dare say to her that all my
former bosses were shipped off with me and that besides, they
were not the types to give paycheck receipts.

(*He taps now on the reverse of the jacket to give it shape and chase away
the steam. He seems to give savage blows but only really does what is
strictly necessary.*)

LÉON: (*Enters, joyful and excited*) So you're beating it in the dark? Ramadier[7] no longer wants any crazies in his government, and

---

7. Paul Ramadier (1888–1961), politician, was the first prime minister of
the Fourth Republic (January 22–November 24, 1947). He forced out the Communist Party members of the coalition government on May 7, 1947.

bang all France finds itself in the dark, happily they left us functioning gas outlets.

THE PRESSER: (*Passing the jacket to Léon*) Here it is.

(*Léon, forming a coat hanger with his two free hands, carefully accepts the jacket from beneath the shoulders, then bringing it into the light, he turns it around.*)

LÉON: Yet another new model: pockets, lapels, sleeves. . . . Well, if that gives them pleasure, and if it brings me orders, . . . (*He lets out in leaving*) I've only got a minute, just enough time to send off the so-called new model with the so-called representative, who I don't like at all, a . . .

(*He makes the gesture of tightening his tie. Simone hasn't budged, she is still seated, staring straight ahead. The presser is seated next to her. Silence.*)

THE PRESSER: (*With difficulty*) He left when?

SIMONE: '43.

THE PRESSER: End of '43?

SIMONE: (*Shakes her head no*) On the Missing Person's certificate, it reads: "Left Drancy in March '43 . . ." (*Pause*)

THE PRESSER: Do they say where?

SIMONE: To Lublin, Maidanek, . . . (*Silence*)

THE PRESSER: How old was he?

SIMONE: Thirty-eight years old, we married late, we were ten years apart.

THE PRESSER: Did he appear more or less? (*Simone does not understand*) Older or less old?

SIMONE: (*Still not looking at him*) Maybe a little older when they took him. He was convalescing. He'd been a prisoner of war for a while at Compiègne. He got sick there, then they released him. Returning to Paris, he had papers made up for him at the Jewish Council[8] to make everything legal, what a joke! He who lived in France for years without identity papers. . . . And at the

8. The Jewish Council was the Union Générale des Israélites de France (UGIF), an organization established by the Vichy government's Office of Jewish

Jewish Council, they gave him a sort of residence permit, he wasn't French, he was still Romanian, in short, stateless of Romanian origin, they placed . . .

THE PRESSER: (*Not listening*) Did he wear eyeglasses?

SIMONE: Yes, but not all the time.

THE PRESSER: And his hair? (*Simone looks at him not understanding. The presser goes on*) Did he have all his hair?

SIMONE: Balding a bit, perhaps, but he looked great.

(*Silence.*)

THE PRESSER: You must know, he never entered a camp. . . . (*Brief silence*) On arriving, the survivors of each transport were separated into two groups. . . . Those who were going to enter the camp and the others. We had to set off on foot, the others, the greater number, climbed into trucks: we envied them immediately. . . . (*He stops.*) The trucks led them directly to the showers. . . . They didn't have time to realize, they didn't enter the camp. . . . (*Pause*) You've been told about the showers?

SIMONE: How can you be sure? (*The presser doesn't answer.*) Everyone says he'll still return, that they're spread about in Austria, Poland, and Russia, being cared for, getting back on their feet before sending them home! (*The presser nods his head silently.*) Thirty-eight, that's not old, not old at all, that they did what you say to the old, to those who couldn't work any more, to women, to children, Ok, we know all that but . . .

(*She is interrupted by the entrance of Léon, who carries a tray on which there's tea, a quart of fruit brandy, and cookies. Simone gets up, puts on her coat on top of her work smock, and leaves after having placed her hand, in passing, on the presser's shoulder. The presser does not budge.*)

LÉON: (*Flabbergasted*) She's one stubborn piece. (*He exits behind her shouting*) You won't join us in a drink? Wait, don't go home all by yourself, at least. Let someone go with you. (*He returns*) She's gone, she's nuts, I think. What's bothering her? If she didn't

Affairs to consolidate all the Jewish organizations of France into one single unit. The UGIF was set up on November 29, 1941.

want to stay, she could have said a word. . . . I mean, asking for an extra piece of work today. . . . If you already agreed, do it in good faith, at least? I would have finished this pathetic piece myself. Did you see that? What gives? A smart aleck, ha, did she say something to you?

THE PRESSER: It was I who spoke to her.

LÉON: Oh good, good. Do you want some tea or a glass of . . . *(He shows the bottle.)*

THE PRESSER: *(Without getting up)* I'm going home, too.

LÉON: *(Serving him)* No, No, I really insist, better a glass of . . . , right? *(The presser has no reaction. Léon serves himself.)* You did well, you did well. . . . I, too, wanted to speak to her for a long time, but . . .

THE PRESSER: *(As if addressing himself)* If one could chop off one's tongue.

LÉON: You're right, you're right: "If one could chop off one's tongue!" *(He cries out suddenly as if he were choking.)* Hélène! Hélène! *(To the Presser)* What can you do? You need a minimum of resilience in life . . . *(He points to Simone's seat.)* That's what she's missing, which explains her . . . *(He searches for the words.)* She . . .

THE PRESSER: *(Gets up)* I'm going home.

LÉON: Out of the question, we're going to drink together. If not . . . *(A vague gesture. He pours two glasses.)*

HÉLÈNE: *(Enters, made up, a bathrobe covering her nightgown)* Has Simone left?

LÉON: Yes. *(He indicates the presser, then in a low voice)* He spoke to her. *(Hélène looks at the presser without saying a word. Léon lifts his glass and offers the other to the presser who unconsciously takes it.)* Let's drink. Drink. *(They drink.)* I wanted to speak to her myself, if only . . . I'm afraid of what I'd say, what words, afraid. I was preparing a nice sentence, full of common sense and human understanding, and something useless spews out. . . . Yes, as if I had verbal diarrhea. It's horrible, it's always like that. . . .

(*He spits, then to Hélène*) Is it that way? Yes it is, I know myself, I know myself . . .

HÉLÈNE: You'd do better to stop drinking.

LÉON: (*Indignant*) Me? I've drunk nothing. . . . (*He turns to Simone's stool and suddenly shouts*) On the kitchen shelves of German housewives, in their piles of soap, that's where he is, that's where you'll have to find him, not in the government offices, not on the posted lists, not in the dossiers . . .

HÉLÈNE: (*Getting up and pushing him with all her strength to force him back into his seat*) That's enough now, have you gone mad or what?

(*The presser has not reacted. Léon attempts to laugh, pointing to Hélène with his finger. He takes the presser as witness.*)

LÉON: Tsk, tsk, tsk. . . . She never had the slightest sense of humor. Never. . . . What can you do about it? A German Jew? Every people has the kikes it deserves . . . (*He laughs*) the dregs of the dregs of the earth, Madame, that's what you are.

(*He makes believe he is spitting on her.*)

HÉLÈNE: (*Shrugging her shoulders and murmurs*) Polack humor! Real refined . . .

(*She yawns.*)

THE PRESSER: (*Gets up*) Well, I'm going home . . .

LÉON: Are you so eager to get back to your bed? Stay a while. . . . Are things so bad around here? (*He opens the window.*) Look: no lights, tomorrow they'll still be striking, you'll be able to stay in bed all day. . . . Thank you, Monsieur Ramadier, thank you, Monsieur Thorez.[9]

THE PRESSER: I can't stay in bed in the morning . . .

LÉON: Why? The strike will be on for Weill, too, you know!

---

9. Maurice Thorez (1900–1964), an ardent Stalinist, was, from 1930 to 1964, head of the French Communist Party, the largest party in post-war France. Thorez was vice premier of the Fourth Republic (1946–1947) and was forced out of government on May 7, 1947, for refusing to support a colonial war in Vietnam.

THE PRESSER: It's a habit. I just can't stay in bed in the morning.
(*Silence. The presser fills the glass again.*)
LÉON: (*Going to serve himself*) That's it, c'mon, let's drink, drink.
(*He hums*) "Let's drink a round, let's drink, two jolly fellows
from Burgundy."
(*He sighs, then picks up the drinking song.*)
HÉLÈNE: (*without moving*) Well, I'm calling it a night and going to
sleep.
(*She remains seated, she yawns.*)
LÉON: That's it, that's it. Go run to the Free Zone, go, go, left to join
her mother, hiding with the peasants. Not me, I didn't want
to, I remained here . . . throughout the war in Paris, Monsieur.
I even had false papers and all, Richard, my new name was
Richard, Léon Richard. . . . Yes . . . I went all over, some days
I was myself with the yellow star, other days, I was Richard
without the star, I even worked a bit under that name at a tailor shop for women in the sixteenth . . . an Italian. . . . People
told me: Be careful, Monsieur Léon, but I thought and so what
if I'm taken, what'll they do to me? Another kick in the ass?
. . . No one at that time knew . . . the blindness . . . the blindness. . . . I even went to play gin rummy in a café with Ar-
menians. And then at the end of '43, beginning of '44, people began to say everywhere that they carried us off to burn
us up, only then did I begin to seriously have the willies, no
longer ways to get to the Free Zone, and there wasn't even
any. . . . One day when I was approaching my house, the concierge made a sign to me not to go upstairs, they were there,
three young brutes of the fascist Militia[10] with their big be-

10. La Milice was a special police unit created by the Vichy government to
serve the regime. Militia members were easily recognized by their large black
berets. They were particularly active in 1943–1944, made up mainly of student
dropouts, ruffians, young Fascists, and poor country boys hoping to "make it
big"—in short, the dregs of society. Suddenly given uniforms and power, they
served the regime loyally and tracked down its enemies. The Jews were its spe-

rets, I watched them come down disappointed, they said a few
words to the concierge, and he hid me in a room way up high,
brought me food and news. There I remained, shutters pulled
tight, living like a mole, endlessly waiting . . . and then one day,
Knock knock knock. Who is it? "Monsieur Léon, it's over, it's
reached the end, the Krauts are on the run." I felt like a tick-
ing bomb had gone off in me! *(A silence)* I plunged into the
street like a damn fool, I had no place to go, I just kept looking at people, their faces mainly, they had of course a happy
look, but how do you say it? . . . *(Pause)* I went from one barricade to the next barricade. . . . Once they pressed a rifle in my
hands, they took it back almost as soon as I had it because I
held it backward. . . . And then I suddenly fell in with a mob
by a truck, a quiet young man clambered up, his arms high
in the air, hands on his head, a young German soldier whose
eyes crossed mine, and I don't know why, I sensed this ass-
hole was wanting me to save him. The men who forced him
to climb into the truck shoved him around a bit to show off
their new military airs. Women made jokes, and the German seemed to cry out to me: "You, yes you, you know, you've
had the experience, help me, teach me." Suddenly I lunged
brusquely toward him screaming: "Ich bin Jude, Ich bin Jude,
Ich bin leybedik!"[11] He shut his eyes, turned his head away,
and sought refuge deep in the truck. . . . Suddenly panic. The
women dragged their kids into the doorways: "Another German out of uniform and that one surly to boot." The Resistance soldiers surrounded me, their leader aiming his machine
gun at my chest repeated: "Papir, Papir.[12] . . . " I attempted to
laugh, a miserable gurgle came out of my stomach, I said in

---

cial object of hate, and their violence and wantonness, their simple cruelty,
brought them general distain. But they were feared for their fanaticism and sav-
agery. See *Lacombe, Lucien*, the film of Louis Malle that captures a *milicien*.

11. "I'm a Jew, I'm a Jew, I'm alive!"
12. "Papers, documents."

the most calm manner possible after having caught my breath, "I am a Jew, Monsieur Officer of the Resistance." I wanted him to know that I was a Jew and alive, that's all, then I cried, I'm sorry. . . . ." The head of the Resistance looked at me an instant without budging, I clearly saw in his eyes that he still didn't understand why I had cried out. No doubt he'd never understand. I greatly feared he'd want an explanation. I drew back. He made a move, finally, and all the Resistance soldiers jumped into the truck, magnificently. The stare of the crowd continued to weigh me down, I spread out my hands, lowered my head, and in spite of myself, my body, my whole body was apologizing. No matter how many times I repeated that it was over, that I was again a free man, with nothing to do, . . . Then a voice, like an old veteran from Verdun, sounded loudly, punctuating each syllable: "In France we respect prisoners of war!" The rumbling of my stomach became even more noisy. Then I became transparent, you know, like the invisible man in films, and I left them to themselves, among people who respect the prisoners of war, the conventions of Geneva, the Hague conferences, the Munich accords, the Soviet-German pacts and the crosses, all the crosses, and I went back to my place. Some days later, the Kraut . . . (*He points to Hélène with his chin.*) had returned, and we laid out our first model in a sort of felt half-cardboard, half-blotting paper. At that time they were not difficult to work, everything came apart like bakery rolls, it was a nice time aside from not finding cloth, or supplies. . . . (*Silence*) And how did they get you?

THE PRESSER: (*After a moment*) They got me.

(*Léon nods his head in agreement. Silence.*)

LÉON: At the beginning I did everything with Hélène, I was the cutter, the presser, the machine operator and Hélène worked by hand. After that we took on the wife of the cop. . . . (*He shows the place of Mme Laurence.*) Then we came upon the crazy one. . . . (*He points to the place of Mimi.*) Then came the operator who brought his cousin, and then . . . and then . . . well you see, little by little as they say, I found myself up to my neck in shit. (*silence*)

THE PRESSER: (*Rises, yawns, and says*) I'm going home. (*He takes a step, then*) I'm not coming Monday.

LÉON: Fine. What can I tell you. If you want your Monday, take your Monday, make good use of it, like the others . . . What do you want me to do?

THE PRESSER: (*After another step*) Look for a new presser!

LÉON: What, what does that mean? What does it mean? An increase in salary you want? Say what you think! C'mon, no games between us, not between us!

(*He is at the edge of tears and holds the presser by the arm.*)

THE PRESSER: I'll come by in the week to put my accounts in order, prepare my account.

(*He places his box of coupons on the pressing table.*)

LÉON: Have you gone mad? What's not right? Has someone become a pain in the ass? Me? Did I say something? Did some one really piss you off?

THE PRESSER: No, No, it's . . .

(*He does not finish his sentence and makes no gesture.*)

LÉON: Give me at least this coming week, we can see then afterward, we're not savages, you know. We can talk about it again. . . . Things can be worked out. . . . Let me catch my breath, Ok?

THE PRESSER: No . . . no, It's better like this. . . . Take care, Léon.

(*He extends his hand.*)

LÉON: (*Without shaking his hand*) You're not happy here, not happy?

THE PRESSER: On the contrary, I'm fine . . . Look! Take care, bye!

(*He exits after having made a sign to Hélène who, having dozed off during Léon's speech, looks without understanding.*)

LÉON: (*Following him*) I'd been warned, I'd been told, don't start with you, never, you're all crazy, all crazy, but not just you suffered, shit, not just you. I, too, I had to do ugly things to survive. . . . (*He retraces his steps and knocks over the bottle and the teapot, he shouts, kicking the table*) Shit!

Scene 6, 1948: Competition

(The workplace. Toward noon. The pressing table is not occupied. Gisèle is working, standing at the basting table. Marie is conspicuously pregnant.)

GISÈLE: *(While working)* I told her, "You can do what you want later, when you'll be married, but for the moment I'm in charge."

MARIE: What did she answer?

GISÈLE: *(Shrugging her shoulders)* Nothing, she was already on the landing, I don't even know if she heard me.

MIMI: You can be sure she got your message.

GISÈLE: Look who's talking.

MARIE: You know, it's normal at her age to want to go out. . . . Once you get married, it's not as easy.

MADAME LAURENCE: Would you like to "go out" in your state?

MARIE: I didn't say that . . .

GISÈLE: "At her age," you know, when I was her age, I didn't go out anymore . . .

MIMI: And you see the result! *(Gisèle looks at her without catching what she means.)* Would you want your daughter to turn out like you?

GISÈLE: I haven't done so badly, there's worse. I've nothing to complain about . . .

MADAME LAURENCE: You certainly don't act your age, that's for sure . . .

GISÈLE: *(Vexed)* Thank you so very much. *(Silence. Gisèle to herself)* To go out, to go out, the only word on their tongues, I like getting home, so there . . .

MIMI: To fight with your Jules?

GISÈLE: We don't fight all the time.

MIMI: Ah, it's clear from here: a hot love affair.

(She hums a song in pig latin.)

SIMONE: *(To Gisèle)* And the youngest?

GISÈLE: Oh, not a problem.

MIMI: She hasn't caught the itch yet . . .

GISÈLE: (*To Mimi*) God! You can be disgusting, it's clear as day you've no kid at home. . . . (*To Simone*) She's doing well at school and . . . let's just say, Knock wood, . . . as long as it lasts . . .

MARIE: What do you want your daughters to be when they grow up?

MIMI: (*To Simone and Marie, from the side of her mouth*) Street walkers!

HÉLÈNE: Look, I'm not complaining but I wouldn't like them to be like me sitting here every day threading a needle, sorry, I say it as I see it, it's not a very appealing life. . . . No, I'd certainly prefer they'd learn to use a sewing machine, it's less boring, better paid, and it's more interesting work, don't you think?

(*Mimi hums, "Mama stitches and Papa sews."*)

MADAME LAURENCE: Sewing machine operator? That's a man's job!

GISÈLE: In the place I worked before, both men and women used the sewing machine.

MADAME LAURENCE: (*Repeats obstinately*) That's a man's job.

MIMI: Why? You need to press the pedal with your balls?

(*Mme Laurence lets out a moan, "Oh!" while all the others break into laughter.*)

MADAME LAURENCE: It's always so pleasant to discuss something seriously with you, we quickly see what's on your mind . . .

MIMI: Men's balls? That's far from the top of my mind. It's just . . .

MADAME LAURENCE: (*Her blood boiling*) Filth, always filth!

MIMI: It's not filth, Madame Laurence, but it never hurts to give them a good washing from time to time, otherwise like all things they end up smelling. . . . Don't forget to tell your husband, when he's washing his ass clean that he does the same with his other organs . . .

(*All the others are collapsing away in gales of laughter.*)

MADAME LAURENCE: (*Covering her ears*) Stop, please, don't talk to me anymore, don't say another word. Leave me alone, I'm sorry for having said anything. Good Lord!

(Mme Laurence drops her work and runs off to the door.)

MIMI: You see! She, too, can use a sewing machine . . .

(Mme Laurence exits, crossing Léon who enters, a jacket in his hands.)

GISÈLE: *(Who has not heard Mimi's last reply)* What did she say? . . . What did she say?

(Simone and Marie are lost in laughter. Mimi works with a serious mien. Gisèle begs her to repeat her last comment. Léon looks at Simone, Marie, and Gisèle, who are not working. They are wiping their eyes and noses as best they can. Then Léon asks)

LÉON: Are you crying or laughing?

MARIE: We don't know anymore. Monsieur Léon, we don't know anymore. *(She moans.)*

GISÈLE: A little mix-up!

MIMI: *(Seriously)* It's hard to keep them calm, I do the best I can, but there are days . . . *(A gesture of hopelessness)*

LÉON: *(With unexpected calm waits for the return of Mme Laurence who—takes her place—and he starts off)* Good. . . . Ladies, give me your advice, for whom are we working, the dead or the living? *(No response. Léon continues, while turning the jacket from every angle—a sad little thing)*

If we work for the dead, I say, this jacket is the very piece for the dead. . . . But strictly between ourselves, . . . a dead person can do very well without any clothing, right? We can throw him into a strip of rags, roll him up, and cast him straight into the hole. . . . We can even save money from the strip of rag and the hole. That's understood, yes or no? If you work for the living, you must foresee that a living person will inevitably make certain movements, like moving his arm, sitting down, breathing, getting up, buttoning and unbuttoning; I'm not even talking about wartime where the living person in order to remain among the living is often obliged to raise his arms in the air and at the same time, no, I am speaking of ordinary movements, of ordinary life in the ordinary creation of clothing. Look at this piece, Monsieur Max has just brought this back to me with a piece of paper pinned on the lapel. I'll read what's written on the paper: "This is work for the dead." (*He shows the paper and he continues.*) It's written in capital letters! Hardly had a client entered . . . (*Brief silence*) that the lining of the sleeve, yes Madame Simone, cracked open, fine, I know that's not a big thing, not worth crying over, things just happen, that's what the seller said immediately, a thread of poor quality, a very lax stitch, whatever. . . . Then the buttons fell one by one when the client wished . . . (*He imitates buttoning*) Then the client, out of habit, looked at the buttonholes, yes Madame Mimi, look at them hard, are these handmade buttonholes?

MIMI: So, what's wrong?

LÉON: They're nothing but puke and shit. That's what they are. He looked up, saw himself in the mirror, tore this junk off his body and fled the shop running headfirst straight to our competitor. . . . Maybe you've heard the term "competition," so you know all the people there work harder and are cheaper because they have less overhead. . . . Seeing his client scurrying out, the boss of the store dumped all the merchandise he'd just received back into Monsieur Max's paws with this little piece of paper pinned on the lapel, and then he, too, raced to get supplies from the competition. Monsieur Max took up the package, looked it over, called me, I looked it over closely and must admit that the client's right: it's first-class work for the dead. (*Silence. Léon picks up, maintaining his professional tone*) Now, I must warn you, those who want to continue working for the dead will have to do it somewhere else. . . . From now on, my workplace is devoted exclusively to the living. And they expect the most today for their money. Those days are over when we dressed them in the worst crap, an overcoat with two left sleeves, jackets that buttoned from the back, etc. etc., it's over. . . . The war ended a long time ago, and with a little luck, there'll be another, who knows, everything's moving along everywhere just dandy. The more we're in the post-war era, the more we're in the pre-war, everything's become normal again, we can find everything, at all prices, they're even speaking of cutting rationing, no more restrictions. . . . I now demand a minimum of professional consciousness, get it, a minimum. (*He puts on the jacket, it's too big for him, and hangs badly on all sides.*) Look at it, just look at this "half size"! One shoulder's already on the ground floor, and the other is still in the basement. . . . Madame Laurence, you must pay a little more attention to your own work and stop looking at what the others are doing . . .

GISÈLE: You're making your intentions clear as day.

LÉON: Clear? Still trying to make fun of me?

GISÈLE: No, no, I mean it, Monsieur Léon.

(*Marie breaks into a mad nervous laugh.*)

LÉON: (*Screaming*) It's over now, enough joking, each piece will be inspected and reinspected and inspected again, and if the stitches are too big, or botched, we'll start again until we get it right. Do and undo, it's always work but the pay is not equal, you're going to learn that now. Up to now, ha, you've had an easy life, now it's over, Understand? Got it? Finished. I now want it to be a prison house for you here as elsewhere, as everywhere as with the competition. I've been a pushover for you, ha?

(*Simone gets up as discreetly as possible, places the piece she's just finished on the pressing table, then removes her work smock, puts on her coat, and reaches for the exit door, making signs to the other women workers. Léon spies her at the door.*)

LÉON: What! Sit down! Sit down immediately! What's going on? What does this mean? This coming and going? Is this a merry-go-round?

SIMONE: I have an errand to do, and as it'll soon be time for lunch, I'm making use . . .

LÉON: I'm the one who decides if it's lunchtime or not.

SIMONE: I informed Madame Hélène that I had to be out, it's important.

LÉON: I don't want to know, I'm in command here, you should have asked me!

SIMONE: You weren't here, so I asked your wife.

LÉON: (*Screaming*) You ask me, me and I say NO! So there! When half the time is spent on errands or taking sick leave . . .

SIMONE: (*Protesting*) I couldn't work one time for eight days in three years, and I even took home piecework.

LÉON: Garbage! If you can't give your all to working here, you can't keep your stool, jobs are hard to come by here, everyday I get requests, there's work here all year long, no dead seasons, you've got to produce or scram, leave forever! . . . This isn't the place to moan, cry, or do shopping, we're not the OSE or the JOINT.[13] I want first-rate work, top-quality merchandise that we deliver and not have it sent back to me with complaints. . . . Who's going to have to swallow the entire line that was sent back to Max? Me! Me! I don't want to hear any more laughing, shouting, tears, or songs from here on out, no one can take off an hour, do you hear me, not one hour, even if your children are dying, even if your old folks are rotting, even if your husbands are bursting with lust, I don't want to know a thing about it, understood, nothing about the errands you have to do Saturday afternoon or Sunday.

SIMONE: (*Exploding, on the edge of tears*) The offices are shut!

MIMI: (*To Simone*) What are you wasting time discussing with him? What do you really expect? Go quickly, don't worry, I'll report what happened.

(*Simone takes a quick look at Léon, he turns his head away. Simone exits. Léon sits down in Simone's place. He remains there an instant without saying a word, as if exhausted. The women workers take up their work in silence.*)

---

13. Œuvre de secours aux enfants, commonly abbreviated as OSE, is a French Jewish humanitarian organization that saved hundreds of Jewish refugee children in Vichy France during World War II. The American Jewish Joint Distribution Committee (JDC or JOINT) is a worldwide Jewish relief organization headquartered in New York. It was established in 1914 and is active in more than seventy countries. The committee offers aid to Jewish communities around the world through a network of social and community assistance programs. In addition, JOINT contributes millions of dollars in disaster relief and development assistance to non-Jewish communities.

LÉON: (*to Mimi*) You have a big mouth, yeah?

MIMI: Everything's fine, thank you, I do what I can.

(*Silence.*)

LÉON: So try to explain to me with your big mouth what she's going to gain ruining her health running like that from one office to another. . . .

MIMI: She has a right to a pension, doesn't she? A single woman with two kids!

LÉON: Her pension is there, there! (*He taps the table.*) If she stays one hour more every night, she'll no longer need to traipse about doing errands, and she'll have her pension, right?

GISÈLE: She can't stay later.

LÉON: Who should it bother, who, it's open, I'm still around? . . .

MIMI: Yes, but when you return home, all you have to do is slip your feet into your slippers under the table, your tea is already boiling. She has to do the shopping and feed the kids.

LÉON: (*Approving with his head*) When you want to, you can. You've got to know where your interests lie. Why would they give her a pension, and for what honor?

GISÈLE: Her husband was deported, wasn't he?

LÉON: But he wasn't even a Frenchman, Madame, not even a Frenchman. She has rights to nothing. Nothing. They give to Frenchmen but not to stateless people of Romanian origin. Who's going to give something for him? Who? The French? The Romanians? They don't recognize him, the Romanians, he left Romania when he was twelve, they don't give a good God damn, the Romanians. The stateless? Ah, the stateless, they can't even give away their heads! They all left with him, the stateless and those who returned, are all tattooed with numbers and all mad like the last presser, you remember? . . . And who still remembers all that? Fresh recruits from the camps appear at the door, who has time to pay off the last ones when there are already new replacements?

MIMI: She went to a lawyer of the Legal Advisory Council who's going to tell her.

LÉON: Yes, of course, a lawyer from the Legal Advisory Council . . .
and who's going to tell her . . .

*(He makes a face that seems to say: "Who am I talking with?" He gets up,
collects the jacket that was on the floor, hesitates, then rolls it into a ball
and throws it under the pressing machine. The women work without looking at one another. Mimi, without lifting her eyes from her work:)*

MIMI: It's not our work that's off, it's his cutting, he cuts errati-
cally. . . . So now is it the fault of my buttonholes if things turn
out badly, if the sleeves are screwed up? Where else will you
find such quality buttonholes? If we had a fair competition,
I'm sure I'd be the world champion of buttonholes. . . . Look,
just look at these buttonholes, I don't make crap! Wouldn't you
say that it's alive, and stares at you, it just can't talk, and I can't
find any braiding, just rotten thread that snaps and makes
knots. . . . Really . . . there are some days . . . I work and ask,
for what good? . . . It must be a lifestyle . . . , I let them yell at
me . . . I've got nothing . . . nothing . . . no nylons, no outfit . . .
not even soap, nothing . . . Most of all, I crave chocolate, I do,
I'd give anything for chocolate.

GISÈLE: What's gotten into you, Mimi?

MARIE: Loaded with jealousy?

MIMI: What. What, I'm not right? The end of rationing? For them,
yes, but what do we have? What do we have, there isn't even
toilet paper in our outhouses.[14] Not even plain toilet paper? . . .

(Hélène has already entered a few seconds earlier. Mme Laurence and

---

14. Rationing continued in France until 1949 on many objects, but food
rationing came to an end well before it did in Great Britain, for example. Mention of toilet paper and outhouses (*les chiottes*) were facts of normal life for the
working classes, particularly in Eastern Paris, the old quarters, where old apartment buildings each had a courtyard where outhouses were lined up for use by
the inhabitants. In those post-war days—as during the war—old newspapers
were torn up and used as toilet paper (*papier cul*: ass paper). American-style
soft "toilet tissue" did not appear in France until the end of the fifties. The joke
among Americans who used French toilet paper well into the sixties was that it
was "sandpaper"!

Gisèle coughs, attempting to warn Mimi, who, having noticed Hélène, quickly curbs her words.) What, what, I'm not afraid to say to Madame Hélène, It's the cutting that's not working, the cutting, not my buttonholes . . .

(*Hélène continues to hang the jackets on the bar suspended from the ceiling. Perhaps those that Max had just returned.*)

Scene 7, 1949: The Death Certificate

(*One afternoon . . . at work, Mimi, Gisèle, and Mme Laurence and Jean, the new presser. Hélène is at her basting table, Simone is taking off her coat and putting on her smock.*)

HÉLÈNE: (*asking her*) Do you have it? (*Simone answers yes with a nod.*) Let me see it. (*Simone takes out a sheet of letterhead paper from a large envelope and hands it with great care to Hélène. Simone goes to her workplace and begins to work. Hélène reads in a low voice:*) Death Certificate . . . by the judicial decision of the Civil Tribunal of the Seine Region . . . on the grounds decided by the Tribunal state and affirm Monsieur . . . deceased at Drancy, Seine Region. Deceased at Drancy? Why did they write down deceased at Drancy?

SIMONE: (*Without raising her eyes from her work*) That's how they do it!

HÉLÈNE: (*Raising her voice in spite of herself*) What the hell does that mean, that's how they do it? (*Simone does not answer, she sews with much concentration. Hélène reading to the end*) Deceased at Drancy, Seine Region, the third of March 1943. What does that mean? He slipped on the sidewalk in Drancy, Seine Region, and he died?

(*Jean, the new presser, comes over and takes the death certificate and reads it. Hélène attempts to control herself. Simone continues to sew with an air of indifference.*)

JEAN: (*After having read it, explains*) They mark the last place where the deceased left a trace . . . a legal one. . . . There, that was the

date and the place of his departure for . . . So that it can be . . .
more . . . (*He looks for the right words*) more legal.

HÉLÈNE: (*Cutting him off*) The date of the departure to where?
Where? They don't mark down that it's a date of departure. . . .
They mark only dead in Drancy, Seine Region, period! . . .
(*Jean goes back to his presser's table without saying another word. Silence. Hélène starts to walk back and forth in the workplace, then comes back to Simone.*) In your Certificate of Missing Persons,
he had departed from Drancy, March 3, '43 in the direction of
Lublin-Maidanek, I didn't make this up. Why didn't they put
that down again? Simply that?

SIMONE: (*After a pause*) On a death certificate they cannot mark
down in the direction of . . .

HÉLÈNE: Why?

SIMONE: Needs to be more precise.

HÉLÈNE: Why? (*Simone doesn't answer, she works with greater intensity. Silence. Hélène shouts out suddenly*) You should have refused, refused, you shouldn't be forced to accept this on top of everything else, you should not be forced to accept this!

LÉON: (*Entering brusquely, cutting scissors in hand*) What's going on?
What's all the trouble about? What's she done?

HÉLÈNE: (*Showing him the certificate*) Read it yourself!

LÉON: What's this?

HÉLÈNE: Read!

(*Léon's eyes skim the sheaf and hands it back to Hélène.*)

LÉON: Good, Very good. This way she won't have to run about any
more from one office to the next. Maybe she'll be able to sit
still here a little from time to time.

HÉLÈNE: (*Giving him the paper*) Read it to the very end.

LÉON: I read it, I read it to the last word, it's fine, very good, all the
necessary stamps and seals are there, it's perfect!

HÉLÈNE: There's nothing that shocks you?

LÉON: That shocks me? Do you really think this is the first time
I have looked at a death certificate? (*He sneers and raises his*

head.) May I have as many orders this winter as the times I've
seen . . .

HÉLÈNE: (*Screaming*) Dead in Drancy! Dead in Drancy![15]

LÉON: So what? Drancy or elsewhere . . . It's just a piece of
paper, no?

HÉLÈNE: You poor idiot, "Drancy or elsewhere," but if that's not
there in black and white on their official papers, with all the
stamps and all their official signatures, look—Tribunal of the
Seine Region . . . Clerk of the Court, . . . Judge . . . registered
on, certified on. . . . Then no one departed from there, no one
ever climbed into the freight cars, no one was ever incinerated, if they just simply died in Drancy or in Compiègne or
in Pithiviers,[16] who will remember them? Who'll remember
them?

LÉON: (*In a low voice*) We'll remember, we will remember, no need
of paper and above all no need to shout.

HÉLÈNE: Why are they lying? Why? Why not put down the truth?
Why not write down, Thrown alive into the flames. Why? . . .

LÉON: A piece of paper, it's only paper, she needs this paper to obtain a pension, that's all. There's a chance she's not even eligi-
ble for a pension, it's certainly not a given right, but she wants
to try, she wants to run around again to all the offices, it's
stronger than herself, she likes filling out dossiers, documents,
papers, it's her private vice, and this paper will obtain her nothing, nothing. . . . It's a piece of paper to obtain more papers,
that's all!

---

15. Drancy is six miles to the north of Paris with easy access to rail trans-
portation. During the war, a public housing block of apartments in terrible conditions served as the last gathering place of Jews rounded up by the Germans
and French police before being placed in freight cars and shipped out to extermination camps in Poland.

16. Compiègne and Pithiviers were towns where Jews gathered from both
the Free Zone and the Occupied Zone were held before being shipped to their
death. Drancy was mainly for Parisian Jews but also held other Jews gathered in
the great "sweeps" or raids (*rafles*) by the French police.

HÉLÈNE: And her children, how will they know? They'll see "died at Drancy," and that's all.

LÉON: They'll know, they'll know, they'll know far too much.

HÉLÈNE: Of course, with you, the less your know, the better off you are.

LÉON: Those who should have known will never know, and we, we already know too much, much too much . . .

HÉLÈNE: Who should know according to you?

LÉON: *(After a moment of silence, gritting his teeth)* The others.

HÉLÈNE: Which others?

LÉON: Don't shout like that, this is a workplace, we're here to work, to work, not to discuss philosophy. . . . *(To Simone)* And you, put it away. . . . Why do you have to pile your papers here, we're not giving pensions here, we're working here, do you hear me? We don't need certificates or documents.

HÉLÈNE: Stop shouting at her, I was the one who asked her to show it to me.

LÉON: And just who are you? Judge, attorney, lawyer, minister of Veteran Affairs and Victims of the Wars? You want to put everything right with your big mouth, huh? Why don't you sort out my problems, mine, and if you find a moment to spare, then you can busy yourself with those of others. . . .

HÉLÈNE: What in the world are your problems?

LÉON: Mine? None! I'm happy, deliriously happy, I'm dropping dead from being so happy. . . . What problems do I have, what problems . . . And who will remember me, Madame, huh? . . . who will remember me? Tell me, who? *(Hélène exits. Léon sighs then starts feverishly putting things in order in the workplace; everyone works in silence. Léon stays for a while in the center of the room, his arms dangling. No one speaks, no one looks at anyone else. To Simone)* Ok?

SIMONE: *(Shrugs her shoulders as if what just occurred didn't concern her at all.)* Ok . . .

LÉON: Good . . . good . . . *(He exits.)*

Scene 8, 1950: The Meeting

The workplace is working away.

LÉON: (*While taking down the jackets hanging from the ceiling and above the pressing table*) Could you stay later this evening?

JEAN: I'm leaving at six-thirty.

LÉON: Six-thirty! So now you're a government employee on their time schedule?

JEAN: Today's Friday.

LÉON: That's right, Friday on the edge of Saturday.

JEAN: I leave every Friday at six-thirty: I have a meeting.

LÉON: You've got a meeting Friday night, and I've got to deliver Saturday morning! (*Jean does not look up, he works calmly. Léon shrugs his shoulders then walks to the door. About to leave, he changes his mind and carries on*) Are you planning your revolution tonight at that meeting?

JEAN: I don't think so.

LÉON: (*Sighing*) Too bad! . . . That would have been a good excuse to deliver the goods late tomorrow morning. . . . Too bad. . . . Then it's only a meeting to discuss, to plan, right? They can hold their talks for a while without you, right?

JEAN: No!

LÉON: Are you such a big wheel they can't even talk about things without you?

JEAN: (*Puts the iron down harshly*) If you want a presser who works day and night to make you happy . . .

LÉON: No one works here to make me happy. . . .

JEAN: Look, we're not a married couple, ok? It's not as if there aren't any other jobs around. . . .

LÉON: (*Taking the workers as witness*) It's the mad cow's disease, all the pressers want out of here. There's something wrong with the table, it leans too much, the iron's too heavy, you want tea at 5 o'clock, I'm a boss who doesn't smile enough!

(*He makes a horrid face like a monkey, the workers protest and suggest giving him bananas.*)

JEAN: Friday, every Friday, I have a meeting, and I leave at six-thirty.

LÉON: Go, go off, leave, may God protect you! You know what? We're going to reassign jobs. You'll meet and busy yourself with the fulfillment of all mankind, and I'll spend tonight ironing and busying myself with the delivery for tomorrow, there, doesn't that sound great? I just want to point out one thing to you calmly, every Saturday that the boys are planning revolution or whatever, I still have to deliver, and I do deliver but you, how many years and years have you been meeting to bring change and fulfillment and I still see nothing that's come of it. . . . No matter how much I look, where's the payoff, where's there any change?

JEAN: That's because you're not looking at it in the right way.

LÉON: Point me in the direction you think best so I can see at last something meaningful in my life. Or give me a date at least: on such and such a day the great change will take place, and the rest of your orders, justice, fulfillment, etc., will follow in thirty days.

JEAN: Monsieur Léon . . .

LÉON: What's this: "Monsieur" stuff?

JEAN: That I attend that meeting every Friday and you can't do a thing to stop me, that already gives me real pleasure, and it's a nice little change for you? Isn't it?

LÉON: Alright! . . . But don't forget to tell them at least that every year I regularly buy the Workers'/Peasants' Almanac and ad space for the festival of your communist newspaper, *Humanity*, at which I never set foot because it always rains then. . . .

JEAN: You're not upsetting me. I'll make sure you'll be among the last to be shot.

LÉON: My wife, too?

JEAN: Your wife as well.

LÉON: Thank you, it's good to feel we're protected. Simone, you'll stay with me to sew the buttons, hopefully you don't have a meeting, too.

(He leaves without awaiting an answer.)

MIMI: (*to Simone*) You're a fool, why put up with that? Why don't you tell him off.

GISÈLE: What? He couldn't ask his wife?

MIMI: Do you really think she'd let her nail polish be chipped?

(*Simone sews, indifferent.*)

GISÈLE: And your kids?

SIMONE: When they don't see me appear Friday night, they'll come looking for me.

MIMI: Then things are fine, if you like it that way . . .

JEAN: You could drop shit on her head and she'd still say thank you. . . . You have rights, you don't even know them, how are you going to make them show you respect?

(*Silence. Everyone works. Suddenly Simone casts her head into her hands on the worktable and breaks into sobs. Everything stops.*)

MIMI: That's it, it's starting all over again. . . .

MARIE: Simone, what's bothering you?

GISÈLE: (*Putting her hands on Simone's shoulders*) He didn't say that meanly.

MADAME LAURENCE: (*To Jean*) Look what you are getting me involved with? "Rights"!

JEAN: What? I didn't say a word . . .

MADAME LAURENCE: Sure, fine, we're not deaf.

SIMONE: (*While crying shakes her head*) It's not that . . .

MIMI: What's bothering you, why are you still crying? Huh? Do you want me to go to the boss and tell him that you're not staying tonight, that won't be any sweat off my back.

(*Simone shakes her head, no.*)

MADAME LAURENCE: (*Rising*) Come take my place, that will make things better, and you'll have a little more air, it's hot today, and it's made worse with these heavy winter fabrics.

(*Simone thanks her with a hand gesture but does not move.*)

MIMI: (*In a low voice*) Are you on the rag? (*Simone shakes her head no. Mimi, even lower*) Were you thinking of your . . . ?

SIMONE: (*Still shaking her head no*) I was thinking about nothing, nothing . . . I have nothing, nothing . . .

MIMI: And why do you need their pension, you're living quite well without it, no reason to make yourself sick. . . . Let them keep their pension, let them drop dead with it!

(Simone shrugs her shoulders with the intention of saying: "It's not that either.")

GISÈLE: It's your kids, they've been fighting again, right? . . . Listen, old girl, when my kids get on my nerves, I'd rather have them crying than cry myself, believe me. Last night, for a start, I got home and the oldest had stained her blouse and just put it into the hamper. She's good at washing things. "Slut," I told her, "You'll just wash it again." . . . Then of course her father took her defense, and then came the cries and screams, I wept all night. . . . I didn't sleep a wink. . . . Oh there are days, I swear . . .

(Gisèle begins to sniffle too.)

MIMI: *(Mumbling while warning Gisèle with her finger)* Shut your mouth, will ya?

GISÈLE: *(Pulling herself together)* What now? I don't have the right to speak?

(She sobs now and makes believe she is wiping away tears.)

SIMONE: *(Tapping the table)* Why am I crying? Why am I crying? I don't even know why . . .

MIMI: Good, then stop and laugh!

SIMONE: I can't, I can't.

MIMI: Tickle yourself under your arm! *(Simone sobs again. Silence)* Ok! Then cry old girl, you'll pee less. *(Simone laughs in her tears.)* There, you see, you're coming around. . . . Do you want me to tell you about the hunchback's poker? All twisted and worn down, you had to touch it to make it pop up straight. . . .

(Simone shakes her head and her sobs double.)

JEAN: *(Getting dressed)* Leave her alone, you're making her nuts with your dopey comments.

MIMI: Don't stick your nose in where it's not needed.

JEAN: If you joined together and demanded to be paid an hourly wage, he'd hesitate before making you stay late. You've got to know how to make yourself respected. Otherwise . . .

GISÈLE: Personally I prefer to be paid by the piece.

JEAN: Paid by the hour, you make by the hour, and the rest is paid in overtime.

GISÈLE: I'd feel less free . . .

MIMI: Especially you who pees every five minutes . . .

GISÈLE: What? I pee every five minutes?

MADAME LAURENCE: Aren't you ashamed . . . really . . .

GISÈLE: There's no shame, I never go, that's all . . .

MADAME LAURENCE: But it wasn't meant as a reproach . . .

GISÈLE: I just don't go, I just don't go . . .

MIMI: Then why do you go outside?

GISÈLE: I don't go out, it's the others who go out . . .

MADAME LAURENCE: That's awful, you'd think someone was accusing you of . . .

JEAN: (*After a brief silence*) You must have water on the brain.

MIMI: (*Showing him the hour*) Better get a move on, Sonny, otherwise you'll be late for punching in. (*Jean exits, slamming the door. To Simone, who is still crying, while working*) Now we can be by ourselves, you can get it off your chest, go ahead.

(*Simone sobs.*)

MARIE: If she keeps it up, she'll smother herself.

GISÈLE: Maybe you want to stretch out on the presser's table?

SIMONE: (*Holds her head up, takes a big breath then between gasps*) I'm going to be fine, I'm going to be fine. I'm going to be fine . . .

(*Brief silence.*)

MIMI: (*To Simone*) Do you want my advice?

GISÈLE: Leave her alone.

MIMI: A good screw like house cleaning from time to time clears out the spider webs and chases away the blues.

GISÈLE: Bah! Another pleasant task . . . As if she doesn't have enough troubles, she needs that, too? A guy would bring her more laundry. That's all. She already spends half the night cleaning the crap out of her kids' clothes.

MIMI: And the laundresses should serve only dogs?

GISÈLE: She doesn't need to take that on, I'm saying.

MIMI: (*To Simone*) Don't listen to her. . . . Look, Sunday I'll take you dancing, you'll pick up a cute guy . . .

GISÈLE: God! How you can be so disgusting? . . . Really . . . there are days . . .

MARIE: What she needs is someone who helps her, who supports her . . .

MIMI: "Kiss me once and kiss me twice, it's been a long long time . . ."

MARIE: (*Cutting her off, really irritated*) No! I mean someone who's really solid.

MIMI: Now that's good, the harder the better. . . . When it's soft, it's useless.

(*All the women break out in laughter.*)

MADAME LAURENCE: (*To Simone, without laughing*) Do you feel better?

SIMONE: (*Wiping her eyes and laughing*) I don't know what came over me. I was fine and then I had the sense of being smothered.

MIMI: (*Crying from laughter*) Yes, it's so, left too long it can smother.

GISÈLE: Oh, shut your face, let her speak. . . . At times I, too, want . . . I want to . . . and then it doesn't come out, like . . . like . . .

(*She searches for language.*)

MIMI: Like what, you fart!

GISÈLE: Like padding, there. (*She taps on her breast. To Simone*) Isn't it so, like a ball of padding that . . . ?

(*Simone shrugs her shoulders, meaning "I don't understand."*)

MIMI: (*to Gisèle*) Hold on. You're not right, you're happy, you have your hubby, your home, . . . your daughters . . .

GISÈLE: Of course, of course . . .

SIMONE: But me, too, me too, my boys are fine, they're doing well at school, here we have work all year round, there are no dead seasons . . .

MIMI: What you miss . . .

GISÈLE: Leave her alone.

MIMI: Come dance with me Sunday, I'll tell my Mickey that I've got to see my mother and since he can't bear her . . .

SIMONE: You're off your rocker, what'll I do with my kids?

MIMI: Even on Sunday they cling to you on the train, well, old girl, you haven't gotten the smarts, send them to play football . . . or go camping . . .

GISÈLE: Thank you . . . so they catch cold, thank you . . .

SIMONE: Sunday is their day, we go to the movies . . .

MIMI: Every Sunday?

SIMONE: Except when it's nice out and we go for a walk. . . . In the late afternoon we go see my father.

MARIE: Grandpa? *(Simone nods yes)* With the children?

SIMONE: I shouldn't?

MIMI: Well I suppose that's one great way to spend a day. . . . If you're a bit surprised later, when can you go over your thoughts?

(Brief silence.)

SIMONE: Here with you . . .

Scene 9, 1951: Building Her New Life

(A summer night. The windows are wide open. Simone, seated in Mme Laurence's place, sews buttons. Hélène, at the basting table, attempts to pack the clothing in cartons causing the fewest possible creases. She grows irritated.)

HÉLÈNE: They'll end up as rags . . .

SIMONE: Where're they off to?

HÉLÈNE: Belgium . . . *(Léon enters. He sits down at the table next to Simone and laughs without explanation.)* It's done, it's finished?

LÉON: Guess what fell into my hands?

HÉLÈNE: What are you talking about?

LÉON: I drew three aces, a black king, a red queen, I asked for two more cards, I throw out a king and guess what I draw?

HÉLÈNE: Two aces?

LÉON: Two aces? One ace! There are only four aces in total and I had three already . . .

HÉLÈNE: What do I know? . . . Why isn't Max shipping this order?

LÉON: (*To Simone*) Do you play cards?

SIMONE: Only a war game with the kids . . .

LÉON: For the first time in my life, I had a full hand of aces but why did it have to be with my own machine operators? Now it's over. If they want to play, we'll play seriously, we are no longer youngsters playing with buttons. Besides, they're my buttons, they really take no risk . . .

HÉLÈNE: Oh, I've had enough, I can't manage, the cartons are too small!

LÉON: So stop, stop, I'll take of care of it, I have to do everything around here, it's simple . . .

HÉLÈNE: That's it, that's it. Why isn't Max here?

LÉON: I have the right to have my own clients without going by Monsieur Max, I'm not tied to Monsieur Max for life. . . .

HÉLÈNE: Are you sure they'll pay?

LÉON: Why shouldn't they pay?

HÉLÈNE: I'm asking, that's all.

LÉON: Because I've had some unsettled accounts you're going . . .
(*He gets up and helps Hélène make the packet. Simone has finished her piece, she hangs it up and takes another. Léon to Simone*) Any news from the children?

SIMONE: Yes, I received a postcard.

LÉON: Everything's fine?

SIMONE: Yes, thanks.

LÉON: Where are they now?

SIMONE: In East Germany, the German Democratic Republic.

HÉLÈNE: Are you helping me or chatting?

LÉON: I can help you and chat, I can do both things at once, I don't have two left hands like you.

HÉLÈNE: (*Looking at him for an instant*) Of course, it's not difficult like that, but you don't see: they'll end up looking like rags on arrival. . . . Roll them into balls carefully while you're chatting. . . .

LÉON: Don't they know how to iron in Belgium?

HÉLÈNE: Fine fine, stop stop, you're getting on my nerves even more, I prefer to do it alone. . . .

LÉON: *(To Simone)* The German Democratic Republic? That's not the real Germany?

HÉLÈNE: The fresh air is very good there.

LÉON: Yes, yes, so they say . . .

SIMONE: They're very happy.

LÉON: You warned them at least?

HÉLÈNE: Léon, will you please.

LÉON: What? I've said nothing.

HÉLÈNE: Just say nothing.

LÉON: It's terrible she knows in advance. . . . In short . . .

SIMONE: *(To Hélène)* I didn't want to send them there, and then I said to myself, after all, if the Jewish Federation organized . . .

HÉLÈNE: You did well, and the climate's very healthy . . .

LÉON: Hmm, Hmmm . . .

SIMONE: The oldest wrote me that they had been taken by bus to visit Ravensbruck . . .

LÉON: *(To Hélène brusquely)* Why are you making up this carton now? Do you want everything to get creased all night long?

HÉLÈNE: You told me that it should leave tomorrow morning at dawn, I specifically asked Simone to stay . . .

(Simone hung up a piece that she had just finished and prepares to leave.)

LÉON: I'll do it tomorrow, stop . . .

HÉLÈNE: We won't have time tomorrow!. . .

LÉON: Stop, I'm telling you.

HÉLÈNE: No, I started and I'll finish!

LÉON: *(To Simone)* Stubborn, huh? . . . Are you going home to bed now?

SIMONE: Yes, that is, I'm going home. . . .

LÉON: You're taking a little advantage that the kids are on vacation for . . .

HÉLÈNE: Léon!

LÉON: What now?

HÉLÈNE: Are you going to stop?

LÉON: What did I say? Isn't she of age. . . . Do we have to speak to her as if we're talking to a young girl by hinting?

(*Simone smiles.*)

SIMONE: You know at night I always have things to do at home and then . . . and then . . . (*she laughs*)

HÉLÈNE: Of course, of course . . . they never realize . . .

LÉON: Who's aware here: You're the one who isn't aware. If you don't make use of the time to go out when the kids are not at home to socialize, meet new people, how do you plan to remake your life, huh? How?

SIMONE: I'm not interested in that at all Monsieur Léon, I'm fine as I am . . . very fine . . .

LÉON: (*Peremptorily to Simone*) Sit down. . . . (*He sits down next to her.*) You know Le Thermomètre, Place de la République, don't you? it's a café at the corner of Boulevard Voltaire and the Avenue de la République, a big café, fine, every Sunday morning there's a lady, Madame Fanny, a very nice lady, who helps remake lives of people who . . . you go to her, mention me, speak to her, and if she has someone, who knows, who fits the bill, she'll introduce him, I mean, if it works out, it works out, if it doesn't work out, good-bye and thanks, nobody's forced to buy, entrance is free . . . well, you understand . . . (*Silence. Hélène looks at Simone. Simone suddenly breaks out into laughter. Léon to Hélène*) What's up? Did I say something funny? Why remain single when it's still possible to make someone happy, there are plenty of men who've suffered and who're alone. . . . She's normal, right? So she can live normally. . . . And even if she were as ugly as sin, with a three-room apartment, it's always possible to find someone who'd be interested. . . . (*Simone laughs more and more*) Fine, let's make believe I said nothing. . . .

SIMONE: (*Calmly*) Please excuse me Monsieur Léon, I have never been to Café Thermomètre, but someone in fact presented someone to me not long ago. . . .

LÉON: Ah! Ah! You see? You see!

(Simone laughs again.)

SIMONE: He even came to my place.

(Hélène drops the packing of the clothes and runs over to sit right next to Simone.)

HÉLÈNE: Why that's terrific, really terrific!

SIMONE: The kids gave him a real hard time, he left, and I haven't seen him since, they were just awful with him. . . . *(She laughs.)* But it was all for the best, because the person who introduced him to me learned since that he was already remarried thanks in fact to that Madame Fanny, and as he didn't find his new wife's place roomy enough, he went looking for a larger apartment, and that's why he asked to visit mine . . . *(She laughs.)* And you know what he said on leaving: "It's a three-room apartment but a small three-room. . . ." I'm not sorry, I wasn't drawn to him at all, and even if I were, I couldn't.

LÉON: So they say. . . . Not all guys are swine, there are good men who are looking for someone. . . .

SIMONE: The children are too grown, they'd be too unhappy, they're used to being the men of the house, and then you know when I got married to my husband, it was practically an arranged marriage, we were introduced to each other for the first time. . . . I must admit I had good luck, I never had anything to complain about, he was a good husband, but today. . . . Its got to be done in a different way, otherwise, I think I wouldn't be able. . . . When this guy came over to the house, I'd seen him once at the other person's house who introduced him, and so when he came to my place . . .

HÉLÈNE: What was he like?

SIMONE: Well, he had a slightly crooked mouth, but he didn't look so bad, he was a man who'd seen better days, and had really suffered. . . . I even had difficulty not to laugh in front of him. . . . As soon as his back was turned, all three of us had a laughing fit, the youngest began to imitate him, he made us go through the entire apartment again with his commentary. . . .

The guy had a bit of a Yiddish accent, my youngest imitated him so well, we laughed and laughed. . . . No, it's too complicated, and then again, you know, I'm really fine with how things are, I feel free, I could . . . well . . . *bon soir* . . .

(*She leaves.*)

HÉLÈNE: Till tomorrow, Good night.

(*Silence.*)

LÉON: Well I laid it out, didn't I?

HÉLÈNE: You and your ideas, really.

(*Silence.*)

LÉON: Ok, let's go to bed.

HÉLÈNE: (*Pointing to the still unfinished package*) You'll do it tomorrow?

LÉON: I'll do it tomorrow . . .

HÉLÈNE: You need a bigger carton . . .

LÉON: No, not at all.

HÉLÈNE: And the letter?

LÉON: What letter?

HÉLÈNE: You know all too well . . .

LÉON: We'll do it tomorrow . . .

HÉLÈNE: Tomorrow you'll tell me tomorrow and the next day and the next . . .

LÉON: I don't have a piece of paper.

HÉLÈNE: Make me a rough draft of it and I'll recopy it. . . .

LÉON: Do you have a pencil?

(*Hélène gives him a pencil.*)

LÉON: (*Thinks about it for a second, then*) What should I put down?

HÉLÈNE: Oh please, we've talked about it and talked about it . . .

LÉON: What shall I put down to start with? What do they use?

HÉLÈNE: "Dear Cousins."

LÉON: "Dear male and female Cousins."

HÉLÈNE: If you insist . . .

LÉON: "Dear male and female Cousins and their children."

HÉLÈNE: Stop, I'll take care of it myself.

LÉON: You want to write it?

HÉLÈNE: No, It's your cousin, write him yourself . . .

LÉON: My cousin, he's not even a real cousin, he's a distant cousin, and she, I don't know her from Adam or Eve, I've never seen her, him, at least, I must have seen twice in my life at most, and I was just a brat, I can't even remember his face, so . . . (*Hélène sighs without answering.*) Distant male and female Cousins, or just Dear Distant Cousins . . . (*He writes*) Distant Cousins. There! Next?

HÉLÈNE: (*Dictating*) If you are still planning to come . . .

LÉON: Hold on! Not so quick . . . Don't you think we should warn them that it's tough here, too, very tough, that they'd have to work hard, I mean really, what are they expecting, why are they leaving there?

HÉLÈNE: Let's not go over that again, they're leaving because they can't stand living there.

LÉON: (*Approving with his head*) They can't stand it any more. . . . You call that a serious reason for everyone to set off and land in a country with people they barely know?

HÉLÈNE: Are you saying you don't want them to come? It's simple: you write them that you don't want to receive them, and that's all, but please don't make me crazy, we've already talked it over again and again.

LÉON: I was asking if they shouldn't be warned, that's all, that it'll be tough here too, that they'll have to work very hard, and not live with false illusions . . .

HÉLÈNE: Who's living with false illusions?

LÉON: Who knows: Perhaps they imagine that the streets are paved with gold.

HÉLÈNE: (*Getting up*) Write what you want, I'm going to sleep.

LÉON: This is terrible. You tell me to write, and when I start to write, you're going to bed.

HÉLÈNE: Fine, write: "Dear Cousins, You will be most welcome and we await your arrival shortly. Signed Hélène and Léon."

LÉON: If it's just to write that, you don't need me.

HÉLÈNE: I want you to write it!

LÉON: Why?

HÉLÈNE: I know you too well, so . . .

LÉON: (*Sighing*) Good, Dear Distant Cousins, do come, we await you . . . alright . . . If you are still planning to come, write us to tell us when you intend to arrive so that we can set things up in the best way possible in order to put you up in your first days here. . . . There, it's fine like that? (*Hélène does not reply.*) You don't like "in your first days here"?

HÉLÈNE: It's simple, if you don't want them to come, write: Don't come. . . . I have a headache. . . .

LÉON: Could I write "Don't come" to my own cousin who calls for help after all they suffered? I simply want . . . we have a duty to them, don't we? Do I have any idea what's on their mind, why they want to leave Poland, why they want to come here, particularly here. Why aren't they going, if you ask me, to Israel, for example? They imagine that we have a giant factory that's swimming in gold and diamonds.

HÉLÈNE: (*Beside herself*) They're communists, they don't give a damn for gold, they don't give a damn for diamonds. They have no family in Israel, their kids speak French, they want to come to France, live in France, work in France!

LÉON: If they're communists, why don't they just stay there where everyone's a communist in fact?

HÉLÈNE: That's enough, I'm going to bed.

LÉON: What? We can't even talk anymore? I was trying to . . .

HÉLÈNE: (*Cutting him off*) Go talk to the wall, I'm dead tired, I've a headache, it's your family, you do what you want, you write them what you want . . .

(*Léon approves with his head. Hélène exits in tears.*)

LÉON: This is awful, what did I say, what did I say? Is it my fault, my fault, if the world's a pile of shit?

Scene 10, 1952: Max

(*A late afternoon. Everyone is busy working, only Simone is absent. Mimi is humming. Enter Léon frantic and running as if he were pursued, he goes straight to hide under the pressing table, behind a pile of jackets not yet ironed. At the same time, Hélène's voice is heard coming from the corridor.*)

HÉLÈNE: But I've already told you he's not there.

MAX: Where is he then, where is he?

HÉLÈNE: Do I know? We're not joined at the hip. . . .

MAX: I want my goods, do you hear, I want my goods, I won't leave without my goods.

HÉLÈNE: As soon as they're ready. . . .

MAX: I know, I know you'll put everything in a taxi . . . (*Max enters, followed by Hélène who attempts to calm him. Max is visibly at the end of his rope, he looks around the workplace for a moment with a haggard air, then he recognizes the pile of goods waiting to be finished next to Simone at her bench, he groans*) But nothing is ready, nothing. . . .

MAX: (*Shouting while pulling together the pieces on the floor or even grabbing them from the hands of the women*) Only the 40, only the 40, I need all the sizes, you've only sent me size 40, I've no use for only 40. . . . (*He continues to collect pieces and place them further away, he moves the pile on the pressing table and discovers Léon.*) Léon!

LÉON: (*As if he were waking up*) Hello!

MAX: You're hiding under tables now!

LÉON: Was I hiding?

MAX: Why haven't I gotten . . .

LÉON: (*Pursuing his thought*) Who's hiding here? Why should I hide here in my own house. . . . I hid enough in my life . . . thank you . . . What's going on? I no longer have the right to come and go under my own pressing table?

MAX: (*Controlling himself*) Léon, Léon, Léon. Why did you say to me on the telephone this morning that you'd put the rest of my goods in a taxi and were going to arrive any minute?

LÉON: (*Shouting*) I, I said that? Would I say just anything on the telephone? Do I even have time to answer the telephone?

MAX: Not you, but your wife.

LÉON: (*Pained*) Hélène, how could you say such things? (*Hélène looks at Léon without saying a word.*) Ok, let's not talk about it anymore.

MAX: I have clients, you know, they're waiting for their goods. I must know, I've been holding them off since last month, last month! This morning one of them came into the store, he sat himself down on a folding stool and refused to budge without the rest of the order.

HÉLÈNE: We can't go on like this waiting in each other's place, soon we'd be unable to do any more work.

MAX: Madame, he, too, has a bunch of clients in his shop who are waiting either for a wedding or a burial. . . . You can't make them wait indefinitely. When you commit to a date, you have to stick to it, otherwise . . . Léon, do something, we've always worked hand in hand, haven't we?

LÉON: Yes, but it's always my hand that does the work!

MAX: I swear to you that if you don't deliver everything by this evening, all that's left, all, you hear, all of it, it'll be over between us, finished!

LÉON: It's over. Fine, there, it's over, what should I do now, weep, hang myself?

MAX: (*His hand on his stomach*) Léon, if one day I have an ulcer . . .

LÉON: (*Cutting him off*) An ulcer, he talks of one ulcer, I've had two already, yes me, two and one gastritis.

MAX: Good, it's over, I put up with everything, everything, except bad faith!

LÉON: (*To Hélène*) Where's there bad faith? I'm sicker perhaps than he is?

MAX: If you were better organized instead of still working in your Jewish way. . .

LÉON: Ah! I see what it's all about, he wants to stick us with an Aryan managing director, with pleasure, let him come, this time I'll leave him the keys and run to the Riviera in the Free Zone. . . .

MAX: Why did you send me only size 40?

LÉON: (*Cutting him off*) Here in my place, that's the way it is: all or nothing!

MAX: (*Continuing*) Just size 40s are useless to me, junk, if I don't have a few in each size I can't deliver, I can't . . .

LÉON: Do you really believe I'm holding back your goods here out of spite? Deliver, deliver, do I have any better goal in life? Any other?

HÉLÈNE: (*To Léon*) Léon, please! (*To Max*) We'll do the maximum, don't worry . . .

LÉON: "The maximum," look around, look! (*He points out the workers.*) All the depressed, the nervous, the unstable, and even revolutionaries squat their tuchuses on my chairs and make believe they work: all of them have a brother, a father, a mother, a sister, children, a husband, and each in turn is born, dies, falls sick, what can I do, huh? What can I do about it?

MAX: And what, in my place we don't die and aren't born? I need two warehouse men, and my bookkeeper wants to become a singer. He practices in my office and drives me crazy and I have to deliver individual allotments, chase after the goods that are doled out in driblets, keep the books, prepare the bills, and ship consignments to the provinces.

LÉON: Of course, but at least you can sleep at night. . . .

MAX: (*Vexed*) I sleep at night? I sleep at night?

LÉON: As soon as I close my eyes, that one . . . (*He points to Hélène*). . . pokes me with her elbow: Are you sleeping? No, of course not, and there we are, and off we go, and you remember X and Y and Z. . . . They just happen to be all dead, and you know how she speaks to me of them, and then come tears, she cries, and she falls asleep, but for me it's over, finished, I can't sleep anymore, I get up, I go to the kitchen, and I shout. . . . I don't want to have anything to do with the dead, the dead are dead right? And those there are a thousand times more dead than the other dead since they didn't even . . . enough! We've got to think of the living, right? And by chance the only living relative left to her is me, and she kills me every night while the others murder me during the day. . . .

(Brief silence.)

MAX: What has that got to do with my merchandise.

LÉON: Who's talking of merchandise here, who?

HÉLÈNE: Léon, Please . . .

(Max, his hand clenching his stomach, is suddenly doubled up in pain.)

LÉON: Look at him, look at him, he wants to pull a fast one on me with his ulcer, but if I just had ulcers I'd be dancing every evening in the clubs doing the swing. . . .

MAX: Léon, seriously, talking man to man . . .

LÉON: Let's talk, let's get down to brass tacks, what, in fact, is our special cloth, huh? A special pure chemical synthetic, is that what you want to make more chic, huh? . . . Do you think I don't know where it's coming from?

MAX: It comes from Switzerland!

LÉON: That's it, that's it, it comes through Switzerland, it passes through Switzerland. . . .

MAX: *(To Hélène)* What is he trying to say?

LÉON: I tell myself that from them we'll receive the shipment on time, never a late train, never a late convoy, the best conveyors in the world, those Germans, only for us, you and me, Monsieur Max, the cloth comes late, too bad, I say nothing, I don't get excited, above all not excited with these type of guys. . . . And when their magic pure chemical cloth arrives, once cut, once mounted, it has a life of its own. It does what it wants, ask them. *(The workers make some timid expressions about the worthlessness of the material.)* Put the iron on top, in so doing, if it dries, it hardens like a board and shrinks, if humid it contracts in length and becomes as pliant and pleasing as a sponge, if you hang it up, it droops, it puckers, it shines, but tell him, tell him, tell him. . . . *(To Jean, the presser, who nods in agreement)* And I have to oversee it all and organize it!

MAX: *(Shouting like a madman)* Fifty percent fibranne, 50 percent polyamide, the latest word in modern techniques, the latest word!

LÉON: *(In a low voice)* Yes, yes, the last word, what do they have over there in stock, tons and tons? Ashes and hair—yes, Monsieur, not worth shrugging you shoulders—hair, mountains of hair . . .

MAX: What's he saying, What's he saying?

(Léon suddenly tears the clothes from the hands of the workers and throws them at the feet of Max, then he attacks the hanging clothing. Hélène and Jean attempt to hold him back and restrain him. Max, panic-stricken, picks up the clothes and folds them while muttering, incomprehensible words. A child appears on the threshold. He's between ten and twelve years old, with eyeglasses, and hardly astonished, finds the workplace in total chaos.)

MIMI: *(Seeing the child, calls him)* Come in, come in . . .

THE CHILD: *(Stops in front of Léon and in one breath)* My mother wants me to tell you that she's sorry but she won't be able to come to work today. . . .

LÉON: *(Screaming like a madman)* And at five o'clock in the afternoon you come to tell me this?

THE CHILD: *(Not at all impressed)* I couldn't come before, I was at the hospital.

LÉON: And your brother?

THE CHILD: He was at the hospital, too.

LÉON: Aha, you were both sick at the same time, now, bravo!

THE CHILD: No, it's Mother.

MIMI: She's in the hospital?

THE CHILD: Yes.

HÉLÈNE: What's wrong with her?

THE CHILD: She can't stand up, she got up to come to work this morning, but she couldn't stay standing, so my brother went to get a doctor, and he said that she has to be sent to the hospital. At the hospital, they said they were going to keep her under observation.

LÉON: *(To Max)* Under observation. You see you see, what can one do, what can I do? . . .

MAX: So that's it. I'm supposed to tell my clients that they can tell their clients that they won't have their outfits to marry or to go to the ball because one of your workers is in the hospital under observation.

LÉON: *(Screaming to Hélène)* What are you waiting for, telephone, send out an announcement, needed, a qualified finisher, without family, without child, neither widow nor married, nor divorced, not engaged in politics and in good health, there. Perhaps for once, who knows, I'll get a good hand. . . . Who needs you all hanging around the kid like flies? You're here to work, right? Or shit, then work, work. Damn, just look at them, look at them, I swear, you'd think I'm already paying them by the hour. . . .

(Hélène has exited.)

MAX: Léon, seriously . . .

LÉON: Don't say a word in front of . . . *(He points at the workplace with his chin. He moves Max along and shouts before exiting himself.)* No one will leave this place before Monsieur Max's order is ready for delivery. . . *(To Jean)* meeting or no meeting . . .

(He exits. We can hear them arguing, then laughter. The women cluster around the lad, plying him with questions about Simone's health.)

THE CHILD: *(Shrugging his shoulders and saying)* I don't know, she's tired.

MIMI: How are you and your brother going to take care of yourselves?

THE CHILD: Take care of what?

MIMI: Eating and all that.

THE CHILD: Oh, we'll get along alright, I know how to cook and at noon nothing will change, we'll stay in the school canteen.

JEAN: That's Lariboisière?[17]

THE CHILD: I wrote down the name of the hospital and all that on a piece of paper, it's in the suburbs . . .

(*Mimi takes the piece of paper.*)

A VOICE: We kill ourselves to bring up our kids. . . .

ANOTHER VOICE: You must love your mother intensely. . . .

ANOTHER VOICE: Always.

MADAME LAURENCE: You are kind to her at least?

JEAN: Oh leave him alone. . . .

GISÈLE: Tell me, sweetie, you've a nice coat on, is it one the Americans sent you?

THE CHILD: It's not nice, it's a coat for girls. . . .

MIMI: You're right, it buttons to the left, that means nothing, you're really good-looking all the same.

THE CHILD: I don't like it. . . . It's a girl's coat.

GISÈLE: All the same, the Americans are nice to send coats to young Frenchmen. . . .

THE CHILD: I don't like Americans.

GISÈLE: Why not, my pigeon?

THE CHILD: I'm not a pigeon, I like Russians, Americans want war. . . .

(*The workers crack up in laughter.*)

JEAN: Bravo . . . for your trouble I'm going to give you a piece of candy.

THE CHILD: I don't like candy, thanks, I've got to go. . . .

MIMI: Tell your mother to return soon, we'll go see her and . . . you could give us a good-bye kiss as you go. Or are you already too grown up to hug the ladies? (*The Child returns, he hugs and kisses*

---

17. Lariboisière Hospital is in the 10th arrondissement of Paris.

Mimi. She slips a franc note into his hand. The child refuses it.) So that you'll buy something for yourself and your brother, too.
(*The others hug and kiss him as well.*)

GISÈLE: What's your mother complaining about?

THE CHILD: She not complaining, she just can't stand up.

GISÈLE: Is she still crying as much?

THE CHILD: Mama? She never cries . . .

MADAME LAURENCE: She'll soon be able to return to work.

THE CHILD: (*Hugging Mme Laurence*) A little later, my brother and I will work, and she'll never have to work again.

(*Everyone approves. The child prepares to leave.*)

JEAN: And you're not going to hug me, too?

THE CHILD: Men don't hug each other.

(*Everyone works with intensity. Gisèle unconsciously sings "Les Roses Blanches."*)

MIMI: Shut up!

(*Gisèle stops singing. Work continues for a moment in silence.*)

On the Way to the Promised Land: A Dental Tragedy

[Vers toi terre promise: Une tragédie dentaire]

CHARACTERS

CHARLES SPODEK

CLARA SPODEK

SUZANNE

AN ACTOR FOR ALL ROLES

THE MOTHER SUPERIOR

MAURICETTE

THE CHORUS

If the need arises, this play can be performed with just four actors.

Scene 1, By Way of a Prologue
Scene 2, Return
Scene 3, The Mother Superior
Scene 4, Without Title
Scene 5, Charles's Soliloquy
Scene 6, At Night
Scene 7, Still Night
Scene 8, Clara's Soliloquy
Scene 9, Bitter Herbs
Scene 10, The Letter
Scene 11, The Moroccan
Scene 12, Stalingrad
Scene 13, Ship at Sea
Epilogue

Scene 1: By Way of a Prologue

(In the home of the Spodeks. An apartment and a dentist's office)

CHARLES: You were talking with them.

CLARA: No, not at all.

CHARLES: Yes you were.

CLARA: About the rain, the good weather, Good Morning, Good Evening, How are things? . . .

CHARLES: Just as I said: How are things?

CLARA: No, no, just words.

CHARLES: With gestures.

CLARA: With gestures? What gestures? Charles, you're frightening me.

CHARLES: These women come in, and right away they're asking you questions with their eyes while they move their lips, "How are things?"

CLARA: They're asking me questions?

CHARLES: With their eyes.

CLARA: No, not at all.

CHARLES: And you just bend your head and wring your hands.

CLARA: No! Not at all. Never, never. Why do you say that?

CHARLES: You bring them into the living room . . .

CLARA: The waiting room, yes, I do.

CHARLES: You slip in with them. You and your ladies pull out your handkerchiefs and whisper among yourselves while you dab your eyes.

CLARA: What are you talking about, Charles?

CHARLES: And afterward, they come into my office with their heads down, sigh when they see me, move their heads, climb into the dentist's chair, sigh again while they dry their eyes intensely, make another sigh, wipe their eyes and sigh again, all that while I have to wait till they deign to open their mouths and shut their eyes.

CLARA: Who likes to visit the dentist, Charles, who?

CHARLES: No one, I know. *(Brief silence. Clara wipes her eyes. The assault has ceased. It starts up again.)* Even less when the dentist and his wife have one daughter deported and the other in a convent.

CLARA: I never speak about it, ever. I swear to you on a stack . . . I never mention it to anyone.

CHARLES: The next time you don't speak about it, tell them that there's nothing new, except from now on, if our daughter doesn't want to see us anymore, we don't want to see her anymore, either.

CLARA: Why? Why do you say such a thing?

CHARLES: So you'll know what to say when you say nothing.

CLARA: Never, I'll never say that. Why should I say that?

CHARLES: So that each of these ladies will stop making a sour puss when she climbs up onto my throne. (*He looks at his watch.*) Who are we waiting for? (*He goes on without letting Clara answer.*) Let them spare their pity and spread it around to others who have a greater need than we have, and above all, above all else, I absolutely want them to stop taking over my waiting room.

CLARA: Are you trying to chase your patients away, Charles?

CHARLES: Yes! I do want a complete change of clientele. I just want to see cheerful mugs in my dentist's chair that don't know anything about our lives or our daughters' lives, patients who don't give a damn about the Jews deported from the heart of Paris[1] to the gas chambers and even—lucky them—about the Carmelite nuns. I only want the former fascist cops with rotten teeth as my clients, or toothless ex-collaborators, or those ladies who wrote anonymous letters denouncing people, so that I can tear out their nerve endings alive!

(*Buzzer! Clara, stifling a sob, holds up a finger.*)

CLARA: Charles, somebody's ringing.

CHARLES: It's ringing, yes, it's ringing, go open it, who could it be?

CLARA: Madame Suzanne.

---

1. This refers to Opération Vent printanier (Operation Spring Breeze), also known as the Vel' d'hiv' (short for Vélodrome d'Hiver), a raid and mass arrest of Jewish residents in Paris by French police on July 16–17, 1942. Arrestees were temporarily held at the Vélodrome d'Hiver, a stadium and bicycle track.

CHARLES: Madame Suzanne and her brat with the wretched teeth? A gold mine this kid for any dentist who didn't know his father was shipped off in the convoy just before the one . . .

(*He bites his lower lip and shakes his head.*)

CLARA: (*Whispering*) You're the one who never wants to make her pay, she wants to and she can, she has a job.

CHARLES: That's it, that's it, I should make the widow of a deported man pay? What's bothering you? Why are you twisting your handkerchief?

CLARA: I've caught a cold.

(*Buzzer! Clara races off toward the door like a little mouse who's just escaped from the claws of a cat.*)

CHARLES: Wait, you know what to say?

CLARA: (*Without turning back*) Nothing, I'll tell her nothing, as I said, we've never talked about it, ever!

CHARLES: Then why is she crying?

CLARA: Don't you think she has her own reasons to cry, Charles? Her own reasons! (*Buzzer!*) She's here. Right here.

CHARLES: (*Moving away*) This bell, this pain in the neck bell gets on my nerves. Remind me to have it changed.

(*Clara opens the door. The dentist has disappeared into his office. The two women at the threshold of the door stare at each other for an instant and for a moment clasp each others' arms. Suzanne brings out a handkerchief and wipes her eyes in silence. They both move toward the waiting room.*)

SUZANNE: (*In a clear voice*) He hasn't come yet?

CLARA: Your son, no.

SUZANNE: He's coming from playing football.

CLARA: He plays football?

SUZANNE: We agreed to meet downstairs, but when I saw it was past the time, I said to myself that he must have climbed upstairs without waiting for me.

CLARA: He wouldn't have done that, Madame Suzanne, he wouldn't have done that.

(*Both of them have slipped into the waiting room. Suzanne then begins to question Clara openly with a look. The dentist's wife, while saying no with her head, nothing new, signals her with a finger on the mouth*) *that she must remain silent. Suzanne understands, then shakes her head, murmuring:)*

SUZANNE: Ah.

(They hold each other's arms again; when the dentist suddenly appears, the two women jump back as if caught in a compromising act.)

CHARLES: Hello, Madame Suzanne!

SUZANNE: Hello, Doctor.

CHARLES: Alone?

SUZANNE: He's coming, right away.

CLARA: He's coming from football.

CHARLES: Ah, ah, he plays football with his glasses!

SUZANNE: He takes them off, Doctor, he takes them off. He's already cost me two broken pairs.

CHARLES: And he sees the ball without glasses?

SUZANNE: It's a real ball, Doctor.

CLARA: It's big, Charles, you know that.

CHARLES: While we're waiting, let's not waste time, come on, show me your cavities.

SUZANNE: I don't have any cavities, Doctor.

CHARLES: Call me *Herr Professor.*

SUZANNE: Excuse me?

CHARLES: I don't like *Doctor.*

CLARA: What are you saying? Call him Monsieur Charles. Don't you see, Madame Suzanne, he's teasing you.

SUZANNE: I always had good teeth.

(Climbing up onto the chair, she suddenly suppresses a sob. Clara does, too, as an echo, turning away as if she were sneezing.)

CHARLES: You don't have any cavities and you're crying? It's my wife and I who should be crying! If nobody has cavities anymore, what'll become of us?

SUZANNE: I'm not crying, why should I cry, Doctor? I've cried more than enough, thank you.

(She sits down in the chair with her mouth open.)

CHARLES: You caught Clara's cold in the entranceway. *(He examines her, then states)* Your little boy doesn't get his teeth from you, all of his are rotten.

SUZANNE: He didn't have any sugar during the war.

CHARLES: Sugar is noxious for teeth. You didn't stuff his mouth with sweets, did you?

SUZANNE: Sweets? Where would I find sweets?

CHARLES: The Americans had sweets.

SUZANNE: And did I know any Americans?

CHARLES: By the age of twenty, he won't have a single tooth left in his mouth.

SUZANNE: Who? My son?

CHARLES: Unless he decides to brush them from now on.

SUZANNE: He does brush them, he does.

CHARLES: Every morning?

SUZANNE: Of course, every morning.

CHARLES: The teeth, too?

SUZANNE: Of course the teeth. Except when he gets up late, he doesn't like to be late.

CHARLES: I can see that. . .

SUZANNE: To school, I mean.

CHARLES: If he misses in the morning, he can make up for it at night.

SUZANNE: Brush your teeth at night?

CLARA: They do it in America.

SUZANNE: At night, he's worn out, he needs lots of sleep.

CHARLES: Fine. When he's twenty he won't have a single tooth left in his mouth, they'll put in dentures. They'll clean themselves in a glass of water next to the bed.

(Buzzer! Clara and Suzanne both run to the door. Charles remains stand-ing next to the empty seat. The door opens. The adult actor, assigned to portray the author as a child, appears. Short blackout. Then the author proceeds:)

THE ACTOR FOR ALL ROLES: Good evening, I am the "author." That is, I'm the actor assigned to portray the author. Here, he's eleven or twelve years old. He's come from playing foot-ball, his mother finally bought him his full outfit. On this day, he had everything but the leg guards, and as soon as he had them, about two months later, he gave up football. Without his glasses, he couldn't even get oriented on the playing field. He ran in all directions but never touched the ball. When he heard the others cry "Heads up! Heads up!" he knew he had to protect his skull with his arms crossed and stop moving. But once, he was hit so hard by a ball, in a strategic spot, a tremendous shot from much too close, that he intercepted it with his middle leg and redirected it. He thought for a time that he'd never be able to pee again. This memorable action for his team, blocking an enemy goal, put an end to his career as a football player.

At that same time, he had so many cavities that he had to spend a lot of his free time in Monsieur Charles's unpleasant dentist's chair. As soon as the drill approached his mouth, Monsieur Charles would continuously bite his lower lip. To tell the absolute truth, the boy was mortally afraid of Monsieur Charles. He kept asking his mother to change dentists, but she would always say, "He really suffered during the war." "But you suffered, too." Yes, but apparently less than the Spodeks. Is losing a daughter who was deported without hope of ever coming back worse than losing a father or a husband who never comes back? Where are the scales that weigh suffering, or the yardsticks of pain? "He's still suffering," murmured Suzanne, while wiping her eyes with her sleeve. So the boy would still have to suffer, a lot, twice a week—because at the time it took a few sessions to kill the nerve endings—twice a week Jean-Claude had to sit in pain in Monsieur Charles's dentist chair.

Sometimes, despite her work duties, Suzanne managed to go with him, to support her son officially but also to comfort Clara surreptitiously and learn how their tragedy was evolving. So that you can really understand this tragedy, that the author by his own admission didn't know or didn't want to construct in classical mode, I must make clear that I incarnate not only the author as a child but also most of the bastards in this story and various other pains in the ass who cross paths with the Spodeks, Charles and his loving and furtive wife Clara, née Davidson. I'll also participate in the ancient Greek chorus of non-dental—in other words, classical—tragedies. The action takes place just after the Second World War, you may already have guessed, right? You've already heard of the Second World War? It's an old story, I know. But at that time, for the Spodeks, Suzanne, the author, his brother, and some others, millions of others, it was still fresh—untreated, you could say. If I'm talking too much, don't hesitate to hiss or boo or to leave as true witnesses of today for whom the Second World War is just endless, boring stories, as the war of 1870, the loss of Alsace-Lorraine, and even the Commune were for the author as a child. People sang, "When will the time of cherry blossoms return?"[2] Today, who remembers this taste of ashes in the mouths of your ancestors? Who remembers the burning bitterness in the mothers' tears? And who remembers those sickly little children, with holes in their chests, nervous, so very nervous. . . . They cry out in the night, Doctor, in their sleep.

—It's the worms
The tragedy, already . . .

"It's the worms, Madame Suzanne, give them a spoonful of the medicine[3] every night and in the morning a full tablespoon of cod liver oil."

Fine, fine, you're right, let's break it off here. I sense that my buddies are getting impatient and that you're all on tenterhooks.

(*Jean-Claude has entered. Clara hugs him, Suzanne grumbles about his tardiness, he is seated with his knees bare and knock-kneed, his mouth open, on the chair of miseries. Charles inspects him, discovers a new opening, a new larder well stocked. He bites his lower lip, then lets out the verdict . . .*)

---

2. A favorite popular song before World War I, a symbol of that pre–World War I period known as the Belle Époque—that beautiful time of peace and prosperity never to return in twentieth-century France.

3. Vermifuge.

CHARLES: When you're twenty, you'll have false teeth in your mouth.

THE ACTOR FOR ALL ROLES: The child approved that and asked, what type of false teeth?

(*Blackout.*)

Scene 2: Return

(*Buzzer, Buzzer. The actor for all roles, in a white medical gown, opens the apartment door. Charles enters, dressed in civilian clothes.*)

CHARLES: Is this new?

THE MAN: Excuse me?

CHARLES: The chime, the doorbell, you've changed the doorbell. It's ugly.

THE MAN: You're a new patient? Welcome, a pleasure to make your acquaintance. I have all the dental charts of my predecessor's . . .

CHARLES: . . . practice.

THE MAN: Unfortunately, I hardly get any of his former patients.

CHARLES: I know why.

THE MAN: Would you please enter the waiting room.

CHARLES: Still in the same place?

THE MAN: I only changed the bell. If you'd be so kind . . .

CHARLES: It's useless. I'm Charles Spodek, surgeon and dentist.

(*Silence.*)

THE MAN: Have you come to pick a fight?

CHARLES: What fight?

THE MAN: I'd advise you not to.

CHARLES: I'm just returning home.

THE MAN: Home? Now listen, this is not the hour or place for jokes, I'm working.

CHARLES: And I don't ask for more.

(*A woman appears. She, too, is in a medical gown.*)

THE WIFE: What's going on here?

THE MAN: Some guy here who just appeared out of God knows where.

CHARLES: From a closet, Madame, a broom closet.

THE MAN: And he claims to be coming home.

THE WIFE: We bought the empty office and the apartment! All the papers are countersigned by the prefecture and the Commission of . . .

(She stops.)

THE MAN: *(Connecting a little too quickly)* . . . the Business Tribunal, the Council of Order . . .

CHARLES: I'm afraid you're not keeping up enough with what's going on now.

THE MAN: *(After a pause, for him)* I was expecting as much. It had to fall in on me. We're never done with them: one more piece of bad luck . . .

THE WIFE: Enough of this. Get out, scram! Get out of our place or I'll call the police!

CHARLES: The police are no longer on your side, Madame.

THE WIFE: What are you talking about? If you don't leave politely, my husband will make you leave. Deal with it, René!

CHARLES: After what I've lived through, Madame, no one will make me leave, not even René!

THE WIFE: If this is the way you hope to make yourselves accepted . . .

CHARLES: Accepted by whom, Madame?

THE WIFE: I advise you to not pursue this any further. Did you ever see such nerve!

THE MAN: Don't try to take it out on the French what the Germans did to you!

THE WIFE: We also had to swallow a lot, you know! Besides, we stayed in Paris. We didn't run off to hide somewhere.

THE MAN: You drop in like this, you pass yourself off as a patient, no no, that's no way to . . .

CHARLES: You have fifteen days to quit these premises, fifteen days more than I had. I'm leaving you the official journal, read it, you'll find it edifying.

THE MAN: We'll meet you again in a court of law, Sir.

CHARLES: Beware: even the judges have changed sides.

THE WIFE: So you say, so you say!

(*Black out.*)

THE CHORUS: The fifteen days stretched into thirty months, despite posted decrees and the intervention of the newly created Service of Restitution of Property for victims of laws and acts of despoiling property. The purchaser in good faith was René Bertrand, a former combatant of 1914–1918, with the Croix de guerre. Finally, with the support of the Council of the Order of Dentists, newly created to replace the dental section of the Order of Physicians, René Bertrand was resettled—a hundred meters away on the opposite side of the street so he wouldn't become an unhappy victim of the reintegration of the Jews.

(*Reciting:*)

Paris, October 15, 1942

To Monsieur the Commissar General dealing with Jewish Questions
1 place des Petits-Pères, Paris.

Monsieur:

I the undersigned, René Bertrand, a former combatant with the Croix de guerre 14-18, surgeon-dentist, with a diploma, 100 percent French, practicing at present in Clamart (Seine) with the desire to occupy an office in Paris liberated by the application of anti-Jewish laws, I have the honor to solicit from your bureau the directions to follow as well as the list of offices available in the 10th, 11th, 18th and 20th districts of Paris.

I thank you in advance,

Sincerely,
René Bertrand
The Commission on Jewish Questions

To Monsieur René Bertrand

In response to your letter of 15 October 1942, I am offering the list of dental offices provided by the provisional administrators.

Please contact with the above-mentioned administrators as well as the dental section of the Council of the Order of Physicians.

Most Sincerely,

THE CHORUS: During the three years of the proceedings, Charles practiced part-time in a dispensary for the Children's Aid Society, rue de Paradis. Clara became a finisher in a men's clothing workshop. During this stretch of time, they had all the time in the world to decipher the exact meaning of the word "deported." Thus they learned the fate of their youngest daughter, Jeannette. They informed the eldest daughter by letter at the convent where they had placed her immediately after the arrest of Jeannette as she was leaving her high school. The Mother Superior had declared that, for clear reasons of safety, she had transferred their oldest daughter into an institution of the religious community somewhere in Spain at the beginning of 1944. She was still there in good health and was doing well in her studies. At the second meeting with this same Mother Superior, they proposed to go to Spain immediately in order to bring their daughter home. The Mother Superior very considerately brought to their attention that the written announcement, no doubt poorly formulated, of her younger sister's disappearance, had shocked and affected her so profoundly that she felt—it goes without saying—the need at that moment to recover by going on a retreat, in peace and quiet.

Facing the panic-stricken Charles and Clara, the Mother Superior advised them rather to write a good letter, conveying their hope, that would help her surmount this terrible and painful loss.

The Spodeks chose to take her advice and returned to their maid's room, Clara forcing herself to compose letters full of hope, which were not answered, while Charles spent more time than ever trying to win back his dentist's chair of miseries.

Scene 3: The Mother Superior

(During the blackout, the canticle "Vers toi terre promise" [Toward you, Promised Land] is audible with the words:)

> The people of God who are dragging themselves across the
> immense desert
> Have fled slavery and hate: they are moving under a
> clear sky.
> They are heading toward a distant land that God promised
> their ancestors
> Where all distress will cease in a calm and serene world.
> Toward You, Promised Land,[4]
> The people of God extend their hand.
> Toward You, Promised Land.
> They turn their hearts and their faith.
> Toward You Promised Land,
> They march despite conflict
> Toward You, Promised Land, Toward You!

(In the office of the Mother Superior: a table, a crucifix, some chairs, the ensemble austere but not severely. Charles and Clara are waiting. They hear the song vaguely, each separately. The Mother Superior enters, still young despite her title. They rise, she motions for them to be seated again. She sits down at the same time and smiles to them in a gesture of a simple and natural welcome.)

---

4. Or, On the Way to the Promised Land. This canticle was sung almost daily in the French Catholic school system during World War II. It is a very well known hymn in France for people over fifty.

Clara and Charles visit the Mother Superior, © *Brigitte Enguerand*

THE MOTHER SUPERIOR: I have very good news of our . . . —your—
beloved daughter. And I am charged by her to transmit to you
all of her fondest thoughts.

CLARA: Thank you. Why hasn't she answered our letters?

THE MOTHER SUPERIOR: She has chosen for the moment to remove
herself from the din of the world.

CHARLES: (*Brusquely*) When can we see her? Or speak to her, if only
by telephone?

THE MOTHER SUPERIOR: She wishes above all else that you may
quickly find calm and internal peace once again. And if I
may add a personal note, I invite you earnestly to turn toward
prayer so that you may derive strength and comfort.

(*Silence.*)

CHARLES: (*Finally*) She knows, and you know, that we don't belong
to your parish.

THE MOTHER SUPERIOR: All the same, the Hebrew people also pray.
Pray, Pray.

CHARLES: I don't pray anymore, either to your God or to my "supposed" one.

THE MOTHER SUPERIOR: I am having trouble following you.

CHARLES: My wife and I are atheists, and I even find the word "atheist" to have an overly religious connotation for my taste.

THE MOTHER SUPERIOR: And you are surprised . . .

CHARLES: Surprised by what?

THE MOTHER SUPERIOR: . . . that your daughter seeks another path.

(*Silence.*)

CLARA: We're not surprised by anything. We just want to see her, to be able to hold her in our arms and cry. I don't see what that has to do with God or anybody else.

THE MOTHER SUPERIOR: (*Offering her a sheet of paper with gray-blue letterhead and marked with a cross*) Express your wish in writing, and I'll transmit it to her myself and give her an account of your visit.

(*Silence. Clara begins to write, then crumples the sheet. The Mother Superior offers her another, also gray blue. Charles walks back and forth. The Mother Superior is waiting. Clara writes the letter, signs it, and offers the pen to Charles, who shakes his head no. Clara then offers her letter to the Mother Superior, who folds it and slips it into an envelope, itself of gray blue, while asking Charles:*)

THE MOTHER SUPERIOR: There is something, Monsieur Spodek, that I don't fully understand, if you will pardon me. You say you don't believe in your God, yet you claim to be . . . Hebrew,[5] no?

CLARA: You can say Jew,[6] my Sister.

THE MOTHER SUPERIOR: Let it be Jew, then. Can one be a Jew without practicing the Jewish religion?[7]

(*Silence.*)

CHARLES: Madame Mother, Sister, Superior, or whoever you are, right now I am far too angry to debate the subject with you. If I

---

5. In French, *israélite*, the elegant way of saying "a Jew" and avoiding saying *Juif*—often a pejorative noun, as "African American" is the "refined" way of saying "a Black" or "a Negro" with their historical allusions.

6. In French, *juif.*

7. *Juif* in French is both Jew and Jewish!

don't restrain myself, I would start to scream violently—louder and louder and as clear as I could be!

(*He presses his fists on his mouth.*)

CLARA: (*Murmuring*) Charles, please! . . .

CHARLES: (*After a time, recovers*) I don't go along with my wife at all, what I want, what I demand, is that my daughter come here right now, look into my eyes, and tell me "Papa, I and I alone have chosen to enter a convent and to remove myself from the world."

THE MOTHER SUPERIOR: She has no desire at all to withdraw from the world, she wants to make herself useful in this world.

CLARA: By separating herself from her parents?

THE MOTHER SUPERIOR: In drawing closer to He who is faith, love, hope, and resurrection.

CHARLES: Fine, let her come by herself and say that to me, I have the right, and Clara does, too, that's all I want. After that we won't talk about it any more. I just want to point out to you, as calmly as possible, that she hasn't legally come of age yet.

(*Silence.*)

THE MOTHER SUPERIOR: (*To Clara*) I shall pass your letter on to her.

CLARA: Where is she?

THE MOTHER SUPERIOR: Wherever she is, she feels from this day forth that she is under His protection. (*She indicates the crucifix with her chin.*) And that is what is important for her today. You placed her with us, fearing for her life, we welcomed her, and kept her out of danger as best we could. Today, her soul and her equilibrium are in danger, she fears cruelty and persecution, she doesn't know yet if she has really been called, she's searching against the despair that drowns her heart since she learned about the loss of her dear sister. At the same time, deep inside herself, she feels a desire to give, to rise up, and to live. She finds herself at the crucial moment of choice between despair and faith.

CHARLES: How can she choose? She knows nothing about life.

THE MOTHER SUPERIOR: The yellow star on her chest, the round-ups, her flight, her sister reduced to nothingness, and she knows nothing of life? She knows too much, far too much, she needs to find a meaning to it all.

CHARLES: (*Almost screaming*) THERE IS NO MEANING!

THE MOTHER SUPERIOR: For you, perhaps, no doubt, but for her? She must find, if not a meaning, at least, some solution.

CHARLES: (*Pointing to the crucifix*) And that's the solution?

(*The Superior says nothing.*)

CLARA: Is she far from us?

THE MOTHER SUPERIOR: At present, she is in northern Belgium.

CHARLES: Holy smoke! How many branches do you have? She's always somewhere else. In 1942 I entrusted a Jewish child to your colleague!

THE MOTHER SUPERIOR: A young girl.

CHARLES: A Jew!

THE MOTHER SUPERIOR: A non-believer. You said so yourself. She will remain Jewish, like you, but her faith and religious identity will be Christian. That's her choice. She prays for you day and night. Pray for her.

CHARLES: It's easy to discuss this with you. It's like talking to a wall.[8]

THE MOTHER SUPERIOR: You are bumping into a wall because you persist in walking in darkness.

CLARA: My Sister, I beg you, arrange a brief visit for us.

THE MOTHER SUPERIOR: Let us first wait for the answer to your letter.

CLARA: But she never answers us!

CHARLES: To whom—to whom do we have to get down on our knees, Clara and I, or beat our breasts with our heads uncovered in order to have the right to see our one remaining daughter again?

---

8. This is clearly from the Yiddish: "m'ret tsu der vant."

THE MOTHER SUPERIOR: This phrase "our one remaining daughter"—doesn't it seem to you a truly heavy weight for a young
girl to carry around on her frail shoulders without the help
of God?

(The canticle restarts with the second couplet while the stage goes dark.)

Scene 4: Without Title

THE CHORUS: *(Reciting:)*

> The Provisional Government of the French Republic
> The Ministry of Finance
> The Department of Restitution of Property to Victims of
> Laws and Acts of Expropriation
> 1 rue de la Banque
> Paris 2
> Reference: dossier: 2196FC
> Paris, 17th August 1945

> To Monsieur Charles Spodek
> Monsieur:
> In order for me to supervise the enforcement of the provi-
> sions of statute 45770 of the 21st of April 1945 concerning
> the restitution of goods sold or liquidated regarding vic-
> tims of expropriations carried out by the enemy or under
> his command, I have the honor of asking you to send me
> by return mail the questionnaire on the back after having
> completed it. The Head of the Department of Restitutions
> Questions:
> > Have you provided a request for contesting invalidity
> in accordance with Article One of the statute 45770 of the
> 21st of April 1945?
> > Have you provided a request of annulment in accor-
> dance with Article II of the same statute?

If yes, before which court of law (civil or commercial) and in what municipality?

What was the result of your legal actions? Please attach, if available, the text of the decision based on the statute.

Was an appeal made concerning the decision of the law court either by you or by the purchaser?

Did a ruling of the appeal take place and if yes, what was it? Please attach the verdict.

Have you reached an amiable settlement with the purchaser?

If yes, have you had it legally ratified through the application of Article 26 of statute 45770?

Do you wish to assert your claims?

The usurper was finally chased out. Charles and Clara then demanded by registered letter—a friend well versed in this type of business had advised them—the immediate return of their daughter to their home and awaited an answer.

Scene 5: Charles's Soliloquy

(Charles is seated in his dentist's chair under a whitish light that floods down.)

CHARLES: I'm with her in the convent, I drill a tooth, and I find myself on my knees next to her with my hands folded. What am I doing? This is not my place, this is not my place. I go back to drilling. The eyes of the patient are fixed on my mouth, I'm trying my best to stop biting my lower lip, I'm causing him pain, he screws up his eyes, his nose quivers, but he says nothing. I suffered so badly during the war, and I'm still suffering. I could even drill a hole in his cheek and he wouldn't say anything, he, too, suffered so badly during the war and he's still suffering. He lost his wife, child, and parents. He comes from quite a distance to share his misery here with me, he takes the subway from the Stalingrad stop, he's so proud to live there. Isn't there a dentist near you with whom you can talk about this? You've already told me everything about it when I worked at the Children's Aid Society and at the health center, why do you keep hounding me? Why do you travel all this way to my Métro stop at Château Rouge? It's not even on the same line. What I really like are clients who happen to be passing through, or even better, the ones who still think they're coming to the honored usurper, the ones who angrily push my arm out of the way without any qualms at the first rush of pain, the first hint of fear, the ones who cry out, who protest—with them I don't find myself in the depths of a convent, strolling in a cloister with coiffed nuns singing their hearts out to "Nearer, My God, to Thee," or find myself in a boxcar with Jeannette, or listening to the raw barking of dogs and the SS. NO, with those who push my arm away I'm just doing my job, battling with fear and pain, two conditions I both provoke and anesthetize. "Stop, you're hurting me!" an occasional patient gurgles. I lift my leg, the drill starts up, I change the bit, then I look him deep in the eye, "Two seconds more and it'll be done," the solemn oath of a tooth extractor. Then, while I dig deeper and deeper, tracking down the deep-seated decay, he winces again, he groans, he whimpers. "Control yourself, don't move like that or I could end up causing you real harm." At least he isn't condemned to a life sentence. His eyes swirl everywhere looking for help. "Be patient, patient, every session comes to an end, every cavity is filled in, every nerve is removed; at worst we pull out a tooth—one lost, ten saved." "Put in a real nice white one, for what you'll pay at least let it be seen." "Fine, spit, it's done, if you feel sick in an hour or two, take an aspirin, don't chew on this side tonight. At the next appointment, I'll get rid of the pain, I'll deaden the nerve. After that it'll never bother you again." There isn't anybody who can get rid of my pain—no aspirin, no laughing gas, there's no end to it, I'm condemned in perpetuity.

(He becomes quiet, then puts out the light and remains seated in the dark. He starts again.)

CHARLES: Condemned to wander in the cloisters or to suffocate with Jeannette in the gas chambers . . .

(Dark.)

Scene 6: At Night

THE CHORUS: Children who've lost their parents are orphans, but there isn't any word for orphaned parents, parents who've lost their children. Maybe there's a word in Yiddish, there must be, and if there isn't, it should be coined at once. We need such a word, especially in Yiddish, an essential word, a simple word, a useful word, a word to call parents whose children are dead.

Nights at the Spodeks were longer than the days, they moved from one room to another. "You can have a hundred houses, with a hundred rooms in each house and a hundred beds in each room, every night you'll throw yourself from one bed to another but you'll never find peace!" The Spodeks wander, cross paths, bump into each other, and even manage to speak to each other, sometimes as two human beings, or almost.

(Charles is seated in his dentist's chair.)

CLARA: What kind of parents are we if the only child we have left turns away from us?

CHARLES: *(reading* Le Monde,[9] *after a pause)* If that's your only question, go to sleep.

CLARA: Go to sleep yourself.

CHARLES: I'm reading the newspaper and I'm not asking any questions.

CLARA: What does it say?

---

9. *Le Monde,* the most respected Parisian daily, the *New York Times* of Paris. It is left of center in its politics.

CHARLES: A Third World War.

CLARA: Already . . .

CHARLES: Already? They've been talking about it for months, years, and suddenly you say, already! (*Silence, he starts again*) Tell yourself that she got married, that she left. All girls leave their parents' home at some point.

CLARA: But in return the parents get grandchildren.

CHARLES: We'll do without.

CLARA: They become grandfather, grandmother, grandpa, grandma, *zeyde, bubbe.*[10]

(*Silence. He reads the newspaper.*)

CLARA: What did we do wrong, Charles?

(*Silence. He reads his newspaper.*)

CLARA: (*She continues*) If we had been taken, you and me and not Jeannette, the girls would have worked things out, the two of them, they would have found two good husbands, and they would have given their firstborn the name Charles or Clara, and they would have told their in-laws what extraordinary parents we were, and their husbands and their children would also have cherished our memory and would even have gone to the synagogue on the holidays to say the prayers for the dead in our honor. They would have lit the candles. . . . [11]

CHARLES: (*Without folding his newspaper, cutting her off*) One is ashes, the other is buried alive. Go to sleep!

(*Pause.*)

CLARA: Do you remember the summer of '37 at the beach in Arcachon?[12]

CHARLES: Arcachon was '38.

CLARA: Let it be '38. You closed the office for a month.

---

10. *Zeyde*—grandfather; *bubbe*—grandmother. Both terms are Yiddish.

11. *Yohrtsayt likhtelekh*—the twenty-four-hour candles that are lit on special Jewish holidays as a memory of deceased parents, spouses, or any siblings.

12. Arcachon in southern France, close to the Spanish border on the Atlantic Ocean, is a seaport, a summer resort, and famous for its oyster beds.

CHARLES: That was in '37 at Houlgate.

CLARA: They never stopped running around, laughing, jumping into the waves. And you, every two minutes were shouting at them to come out of the water. "They don't know how to swim and neither do I!" You were always afraid, Charles, always.

CHARLES: Yes. That's how I thought of my job as a father: constantly fearful, never being taken by surprise, always expecting the worst.

CLARA: And the worst of the worst has befallen us. (*Silence.*) I was afraid, too, you know. (*Silence.*) Afraid for them, always.

CHARLES: If love is measured in terms of the fear that parents have for their children, no child in this world was ever more intensely loved than ours.

(*Silence. He picks up his newspaper and disappears behind it.*)

CLARA: Charles?

(*He does not answer.*)

CLARA: If we did as the Sister suggested.

CHARLES: What sister? What are you still talking to me about?

CLARA: The Mother Superior.

CHARLES: What did she say?

CLARA: To pray.

CHARLES: To pray?

CLARA: If we'd go back there and said we wanted to become . . . and later asked if that could let us get closer to . . .

CHARLES: (*Throwing down his newspaper on the ground*) What are you saying? What are you saying?

CLARA: Don't shout, I'm only saying: If we already believe in nothing, then why not . . .

CHARLES: (*Cutting her off*) Ah, excuse me, we believe, we believe!

CLARA: What do we believe in Charles?

CHARLES: In that!

CLARA: In that what?

CHARLES: We believe that we don't believe. That's all. That's what we believe in, that's our faith, our religion: not to believe! And every day I believe in it more. And what are you trying to make me say? What are you trying to make me say? We are Jews, Clara, Jews, do you know what that is? Do you know what that means?

CLARA: In any case she said that you can still stay Jews even while becoming . . .

CHARLES: (*Suddenly*) Clara go to sleep! Go to sleep! Leave me alone! Leave me alone! Let me hope for the Third World War with a minimum of calm and serenity!

CLARA: Charles, we're talking.

CHARLES: NO, not at all, go to sleep! Go to sleep before I really begin to scream!

CLARA: Charles, the neighbors are sleeping.

CHARLES: So what? Do you really think I'm afraid of waking them? Afraid? They were also sleeping when the cops and their little Gestapoettes climbed up the stairs to our apartment, right? Your neighbors! The entire world was asleep! Do you want me to open the window and begin to shout?

CLARA: It's impossible to talk with you.

CHARLES: Right. You can't talk, especially if you're going to say a lot of crap.

CLARA: Charles . . .

CHARLES: Pure crap! You made yourself clear, very clear, you were suggesting that I should convert, that I, of all people, should convert! You think because I don't believe in some sort of God, I can renounce my convictions like *that*? Making such a swift change pits the Old Testament against their new one? No one in my family, no one ever converted, ever.

CLARA: But they were believers, Charles, we . . .

CHARLES: No one in my family ever did, ever, ever! Do you understand?

CLARA: Not in my family either! What do you think?

(*They stop talking, the canticle in sotto voce fills the void, little by little in spurts. Suddenly, Clara gets up and retreats to her bedroom repressing a sob.*)

CHARLES: That's it, that's it.

(He climbs back up into his dentist's chair, spreads out Le Monde *on his face, and tries to fall asleep. The canticle dissolves into silence and the voice of Clara is heard.)*

CLARA: Come to bed, I won't say any more. . . . It was just something to talk about, come . . .

(Charles does not move, the silence increases.
Dark.)

Scene 7: Still Night

THE CHORUS: So as not to frustrate further any readers or spectators who are avid for theological controversies or who seek a precise and concise definition answering the question "What is a Jew?"—above all, for those who claim to be nonbelievers—the author provides two observations. One has been attributed to Jean-Paul Sartre: "A Jew is one who does not deny that he is, if he is." Fine. The other is drawn from a brochure published pseudonymously at the author's expense in Warsaw around 1912 in Russian and Esperanto but never distributed. The brochure was edited by Dr. Lazare Zamenhof, an ophthalmologist, ex-Zionist militant, and creator and promoter of Esperanto: "Persecute the Jews as much as you want, their Jewishness as such will not disappear; make atheists of all the Jews, their Jewishness will not disappear and all these atheists will continue to call themselves Jews." In the end, to clarify definitively for slow learners, here is a proverbial definition with a Yiddish flavor dating from before the catastrophe: "A Jew is easy to recognize: he has a head, two eyes, a nose, a mouth, two ears, and above all, he speaks Yiddish. Even the youngest speaks Yiddish, which proves for those who still doubt it that of all the languages of the Earth, Yiddish is the easiest to learn and to speak." That's it. For further details, consult Google or any other lending library at the shelf marked "Judaica/Hebraica." Expect to spend a lot of free time just absorbing the various layers of meaning from the shelves devoted to the Jewish Question before attempting to clarify them. Meanwhile, let's return to the depths of the night at Métro station Château Rouge, where the Spodeks are lost in thought and roam about.

Scene 8: Clara's Soliloquy

(*We find Charles again spread out on his dentist's throne, his face covered by* Le Monde, *as we left him before the introduction of the Chorus. Clara enters in her nightgown, she murmurs in the half-light of dawn . . .*)

CLARA: Charles, Charles, are you sleeping, are you sleeping?
(*Nothing moves. She sits down not far from the throne and remains silent, then . . .*)

CLARA: You know, I know why, yes, yes. I know. I understand her, and in spite of myself I approve of her decision. She is seeking a path, her path, to meet up with Jeannette, not to abandon her, not to leave her alone in the boxcar or under the gas. She needs to believe, yes, to believe that one day they will find themselves again in a world, how can I say it, a better world? Another world? Yes, she found a path that brings her closer to Jeannette but inevitably takes her away from us. Like Jeannette, she will never be a woman, she will never know carnal love, she will remain a virgin forever, like Jeannette her hair—her long hair—will be close-cropped, sheared. She can't come to us and cry in our arms for her, no, she can't. She knows that here in this house, inside these walls, the word "death" is final, without recourse, without escape. For us here, ashes are ashes and will remain ashes forever. She's found a refuge, a place where death is only temporary, a place where resurrection is assured, a temporary place, transitory, a place where grace rules. Sheltered inside its high walls, she waits. She's afraid, afraid to see our pain, afraid to read on our faces the reality that Jeannette, her Jeannette, our Jeannette, is dead, dead, dead, reduced to smoke, belched up and dissolved in the freezing sky of Poland.

(*Silence.*)

CLARA: And no doubt, she holds it against us, and against herself. Jeannette is dead, her sister, our daughter, is dead and we're alive, we're alive, all three of us, alive despite everything. She's punishing us for that, in spite of herself, and she's punishing herself, too. Pleasure, even the slightest pleasure, is forbidden during this period of mourning, and like our mourning, for all three of us, it is endless. There will never be any pleasure, not for her and not for us. Wherever we are, wherever she is, there'll always be pain.

And what would she do with us at home? She'd go back to school, meet with kids of other deported parents during the day, but at night she'd wander like a soul in pain, like us, Charles, from one room to the other throughout the night without finding any rest. There, behind thick walls, where grace is spread widely, she rises before dawn, repeats the same motions, the same words, whispers the same prayers, "Hail Mary, full of grace," perhaps she even sings with the others "On the Way to Jerusalem."

This way, at every moment, she can be near Jeannette, obliterate the atrocity, the barbarity, deny the horror . . . to wait, to hope for the moment when, in another world, they'll find each other again and go back to their childlike games. It's only there, when they're united again, that they'll remember Charles and Clara, their beloved parents. You know, it happens to me, too—yes, really—despite myself, like a burst, a burst of prayer.

(*Silence.*)

CLARA: Wherever You are, whoever You are, the next time You make a world, consider, I beg You, consider, think about human beings who have to live there.

(*Charles moves suddenly,* Le Monde *falls to the floor, he draws up and asks, discovering Clara at his feet:*)

CHARLES: What are you doing there?

CLARA: I'm praying.

(He stares at her bewildered, then descends with effort from his throne. He does not pick up Le Monde *and makes his way to his bedroom, feeling his way.)*

CLARA: And what are you doing?

CHARLES: I'm going to go to bed.

CLARA: It'll soon be time to get up!

(He disappears. She remains alone for an instant and then draws herself up. It is already daylight. She approaches the window and remains there. She calls out to Charles as the stage goes dark:)

CLARA: It's going to be another nice day.

Scene 9: Bitter Herbs

(Buzzer! Charles appears in a white medical gown. He questions Clara, who removes his medical apron and combs her hair hastily:)

CHARLES: It's them?

CLARA: Who do you expect it to be? Not a patient at this hour.

CHARLES: Even a patient with his mouth wide open finally shuts up, but *he* can't stop talking even with his mouth full.

CLARA: He's your cousin, not mine. *(Buzzer)* They're here, they're here. Take off your gown.

CHARLES: And if it were a patient?

CLARA: Charles!

(He goes into his office, removes the gown, while Clara welcomes a well-dressed couple, Max and Mauricette.)

MAX: *(Acting a bit fussy)* Clara, Clara, we can kiss, ok?

CLARA: We can kiss, Max.

MAX: We see each other once in a blue moon, but the feeling is there, isn't it? Where's the great man? Still fiddling with other people's teeth?

CLARA: He's changing his clothes.

MAX: Business booming? Lots of rotting teeth?

CLARA: There's no cash flowing, but there are plenty of teeth decaying.

Mauricette, Charles, Max, and Clara, © *Brigitte Enguerand*

MAX: Well, well, look, I managed to find us a bottle of kosher Bordeaux.

(Mauricette and Clara embrace one another. Mauricette offers a little flower bouquet to Clara.)

CLARA: That wasn't necessary, Mauricette . . .

(Charles enters.)

MAX: Charles, my good Charles.

(They come toward one another and kiss each other on both cheeks in the French style, then Charles's lips graze the cheeks of Mauricette.)

MAX: *(Extending his bottle to Charles)* I don't want to make it an order, but it would be better to open it before the meal so the wine can breathe.

CLARA: It's kosher wine.

CHARLES: Then it should breathe even bottled up!

MAX: *(Addressing himself to Clara)* For such an evening, it seemed necessary, don't you think?

(Clara approves.)

MAURICETTE: *(To Clara)* You're going to laugh, but I was on the verge of inviting you to our place, we wanted to make a big production with the kids, but then I thought it would be better . . .

MAX: (*Rushing to her support*) . . . to make it an informal gathering, yes, yes, that's it, I was touched that you thought to invite us on such a night as this.

CHARLES: A Wednesday?

MAX: Ah, ah, a Wednesday!

MAURICETTE: The first night of Passover.

CLARA: Ah, yes, yes, yes . . .

MAX: We said to each other, they are inviting us to a seder at their home, let's go, we can't refuse, can we? We canceled ours with the kids . . .

CLARA: You keep kosher?

MAURICETTE: Not every day but for the holidays . . .

CHARLES: Are you believers?

MAURICETTE: We couldn't say that, but we respect the traditions, especially for the children and the grandchildren.

MAX: Otherwise everything will disappear, and Hitler will have won.

CHARLES: In my house he's already won.

(*Silence.*)

CLARA: Do you want to drink something?

MAX: No, we can say kiddush first.

CHARLES: I'm going to wash my hands.

(*He leaves, Max takes out his kippah and places it on his head.*)

CLARA: (*Very annoyed*) We have nothing for . . .

MAX: I took care of it all, even the bitter herbs.

CLARA: We didn't know, we don't know at all anymore how people live. . . . The dates of the holidays, all that . . . Better not start, Max, better not start. Excuse me, Mauricette, but . . . sit down, the hors d'oeuvres are on the table, he'll be back soon. Ah, I don't even have any matzah.

(*They sit down in silence. Charles returns, Max quickly removes his kippah and arranges the bitter herbs. Silence. Charles takes the bottle and goes out again. All three are seated. Charles returns and places the uncorked bottle down solidly on the table, then seats himself, and while spreading out his napkin, he asks Clara:)*

CHARLES: Finished?

CLARA: Excuse me?

CHARLES: Their . . .

(Clara nods yes. Max and Mauricette glance at one another.)

CLARA: *(Finally)* Good, ah, It's time to eat. Serve yourself, or I can serve you. *(She adds, most unhappily)* It's not quite kosher, if you don't want any ham . . .

CHARLES: *(Cutting her off)* Stop! I'm a specialist. Pig ham, I baptize goose ham, there, now you can it eat.

MAURICETTE: *(Laughing, irritated)* But who's eating kosher? It's only on Jewish holidays, and even then . . . !

MAX: And even then it's very, very rare, yes, yes.

(They serve themselves.)

MAX: *(To calm the atmosphere)* Guess who just passed away?

CHARLES: Now or a few years ago?

MAX: Just now.

CHARLES: I didn't see anyone I knew in *Le Monde*.

CLARA: Blumberg?

MAX: No, no, but he's very very sick.

CLARA: I was just saying . . .

MAX: No, no, he's really bad, near the end of his rope but still hanging on. You'll never guess, Tannenbaum!

CHARLES: The chairman?

MAX: The chairman.

CHARLES: Roger?

MAX: Yes, Roger.

MAURICETTE: What Roger and what chairman are you talking about?

MAX: Roger Tannenbaum, the chairman of the Universal Brotherhood.

MAURICETTE: You never told me.

MAX: Did you know him?

MAURICETTE: Who? Tannenbaum? No.

MAX: Charles and I knew Tannenbaum well, he was a bit older than us, wasn't he?

CHARLES: Hardly.

MAX: The generation between ours and our parents'. *(Silence)* He survived everything, really everything, and then, in less than fifteen days, packed up, and shipped off.

CLARA: Was he poorly taken care of?

MAX: What do you think? He had the best doctors.

CHARLES: Absolutely.

MAX: No, his time had come, that's all. When it's your hour . . . *(They eat in silence. Then to Charles)* So what's up?

CHARLES: What's up?

MAX: What's going on with you?

(Silence.)

CLARA: Nothing's changed.

(Short silence.)

MAX: *(Drawing himself up)* You know, Charles, I've never wanted to give you the least bit of advice, you're a seasoned fellow, a graduate of the School of Dentistry, and more, but you really must hire a lawyer.

CLARA: *(Frightened stiff)* A lawyer?

MAX: You must hire a lawyer.

CHARLES: Just what I need, to take my daughter to court?

MAX: Whose talking about taking your daughter to court? You subpoena the Mother Superior and the convent for non-restitution of a child.

CHARLES: She's nineteen years old, soon she'll be twenty.

(Silence.)

MAX: You hire a lawyer, and you give them hell, believe me. *(Silence)* If you don't want a lawyer, at least go to Kaplan, the Grand Rabbi of France,[13] or Oscar Breiner, Mauricette's un-

---

13. Jacob Kaplan (1895–1994) was the Grand Rabbi of France (1955–1981). He sought good relations with the Catholic Church and other Christian groups. Born in Paris, he served in World War I and was active during World War II

cle, who played gin rummy with him every Thursday before the war.

CLARA: Kaplan the Rabbi?

MAX: The Grand Rabbi, yes, ever since he became involved with the Finaly children, you saw the rumpus it caused.[14]

MAURICETTE: He went straight to the Archbishop.

MAX: And he can go even higher, much much higher without any intermediary. He picks up the phone and . . .

(Silence. Charles grinds his teeth.)

CLARA: What can we lose, Charles?

(Silence, then:)

CHARLES: I don't want to cause a scene, I don't want it to become a theological battle between the Grand Rabbi and the Archbishop, I want her to return by herself if she wants to, and that's that!

MAURICETTE: But suppose they're keeping her by force?

CHARLES: At nineteen?

CLARA: She was only fourteen when . . .

---

with the Underground. He denounced the Vichy government's anti-Judaic laws publicly. After the war, he dealt with many problems related to the Holocaust and its victims. He was involved with the Finaly family and restoring the orphaned children to their Jewish family from the grasp of the Catholic Church.

14. The Finaly Affair—upon which much of this play is based—took place in the early 1950s. The two Finaly children, Robert (1941–) and Gerald (1942–), were orphaned Jewish children whose French Jewish parents were deported and killed. The Church baptized the children and refused to return them to the surviving aunts and uncles of the Finaly family, who took their case to the French courts and finally won the right to have the children restored to their Jewish family. It was one of the rare cases in which, out of hundreds of deceitfully baptized Jewish children, the children were returned to their Jewish families. In 1953, in the time period of the play, the Finaly children were finally passed to their Jewish family by order of the French court and through the negotiations of Grand Rabbi Jacob Kaplan with the Catholic Church. The aftermath of the affair seared a generation of French Jews and many French Republicans. It was a victory of secular French law over Catholic Church canon law in the Fourth Republic of France.

CHARLES: At nineteen or even fourteen, she knows our address, her address, she can come home if she wants to or write.

CLARA: Suppose she doesn't even know if we're alive? Maybe she never received our letters?

CHARLES: Clara, Stop! Wherever she is, she can come here and find out if we're dead or alive.

CLARA: Perhaps she came by when it was occupied by the Bertrands and . . .

MAURICETTE: Perhaps the nuns stopped her from leaving?

(*Charles hits the table shouting.*)

CHARLES: IS THERE NO DESSERT?

CLARA: Charles, we haven't even eaten the main course yet.

CHARLES: Then what are you waiting for, the Flood?

(*Clara gets up, clears the table, and goes to the kitchen. Mauricette removes the last plates and follows her.*)

MAURICETTE: I'll help you.

CLARA: It's not necessary, I just have one dish to take out of the oven.

MAURICETTE: I'm going to help you.

(*Both of them flee. Silence.*)

CHARLES: (*Offering his wine glass abruptly to Max*) I'll gladly take a drop of your kosher wine.

(*Max serves him, then:*)

MAX: Charles, you're not being reasonable. (*Charles finishes drinking. Max continues while serving himself*) We can never get to the bottom of things, you don't listen to any advice . . .

CHARLES: Certainly not when you enter my house and pester me with stupid stories.

MAX: Charles!

CHARLES: Hire a lawyer, go see a Rabbi, every time I see you it's always the same story. I'm waiting for the day when you'll send me to your fortune teller.

MAX: Charles, excuse me, but I won't let you speak to me in that tone.

CHARLES: You won't? What are you going to do about it? Send me to your Rabbi, your lawyer?

(*Max gets up.*)

MAX: I could punch you in the mouth!

CHARLES: (*Getting up and standing his ground*) Why not, with pleasure, for years now I've looked forward to doing this with the greatest desire, go ahead, go ahead, punch me in the mouth!

(*Max remains standing facing Charles, both of their arms swinging.*)

MAX: Charles, I know how much you're suffering, but there's . . .

CHARLES: Stop going on about my suffering, punch me in the mouth so I can suffer for a reason!

(*The two women enter. Clara carries a casserole taken from the oven, Mauricette holds the table mat.*)

MAURICETTE: (*With a false sprightliness*) The main course!

MAX: Let's leave, we're going home; his grief is driving him crazy.

CHARLES: (*Sneering*) Promises, ha? Always promises . . .

CLARA: What promises, Charles?

CHARLES: He plans to punch me in the mouth but then stands there like a shriveling coward. Go ahead, go ahead, without a lawyer, without a Rabbi, punch me in the mouth!

MAURICETTE: Charles, you shouldn't talk that way on a night like this!

CHARLES: What do you mean on a night like this?

MAX: (*To Mauricette*) Come on, let's go home, excuse me Clara, but . . .

(*Clara places the casserole down on the table.*)

MAURICETTE: (*Waving the table mat, shouts*) You're going to burn the tablecloth!

(*Charles sits down.*)

CHARLES: Great! This little scene has given me an appetite, are you planning to eat or leave?

(*Silence. After a short hesitation, all three sit down again in silence. Clara serves everyone. They begin to eat. Little by little Max and Mauricette savor the dish and make it known by grunting with satisfaction. Blackout. Then a feminine voice or feminine presence announces:*)

THE VOICE: A little footnote concerning the children of the Finaly Affair. The two sons of Doctor Finaly and his wife, both dead during the deportation, were placed in the home of a certain

Madame Brun in 1943. She had them baptized in 1945 and therefore refused to return the kids to the survivors of the Finaly family who reclaimed them after they'd traced them down despite many obstacles. It was only after the Grand Rabbi Joseph Kaplan, pressed by a committee of supporters and a tough newspaper campaign, intervened directly to the highest Catholic authorities, that the return of the Finaly children was possible. After many years of theological proceedings and confrontations, the children were returned—in 1953, to be exact—to their family and to Judaism. Those are the facts. Now let's return to the Spodeks. Max and Mauricette have left, promising to start again next year with a real seder, this time with children, grandchildren, the four questions, answers, and so forth.

(Clara closes the door and remains in the corridor for a moment.)

CHARLES: *(Violently pushing his plate aside)* Never invite anybody ever again!

CLARA: I thought it would give you some pleasure.

CHARLES: You know what would give me some pleasure?

CLARA: I know, I know. *(Silence. She continues)* What's stopping you from doing it, you know the doses and the substances?

CHARLES: Laughing gas in a lethal dose: literally make yourself laugh to death?

CLARA: What an idea!

CHARLES: Who'll give me the injection?

CLARA: I would, if that's what you want.

CHARLES: And who'll give it to you?

CLARA: Why me? *(Silence)* I have to stay behind to deal with your funeral and sell off the office . . .

CHARLES: And give everything to the Sisters of Charity! No, no, I don't want to do to myself what Hitler didn't succeed in doing to me. I'll wait.

CLARA: Wait for what?

CHARLES: My time. *(Silence. Reading the label on the bottle of kosher wine)* Blessed are You, Eternal God, King of the Universe, who created the fruit of the vine.

CLARA: What are you saying?

CHARLES: Nothing. I'm reading the label: Bordeaux superior certified kosher.

CLARA: You still remember the Passover prayers?

(Charles searches then:)

CHARLES: Blessed are You, Oh Eternal God, who sanctifies us by your commandments and orders us to eat bitter herbs, bitter herbs . . .

CLARA: Blessed are You, our God, who brought us forth from Egypt where the Pharaoh had reduced us to slavery. *(Silence)* Is it after that that we say: Next year in Jerusalem?

(Charles raises his shoulders in a sign of indifference or of ignorance.)

CLARA: Then: Next year . . .

CHARLES: . . . in Jerusalem or elsewhere, together.

(He places his hand on Clara's. Blackout.)

Scene 10: The Letter

THE CHORUS:

20 July 1953

Most dear Parents:

A few days ago, I became Sister Maria-Teresa of the Order of the Resurrection of Christ. I have thought a lot about you. I think about you often, about your sadness, your pain, and your confusion. I pray for you, pardon me, but I can only do that. I pray for Jeannette. She remains and will remain in my heart forever. Tomorrow or in a few days I will be going off far away, very far, to a country where children are dying and parents are suffering. Wherever children are crying, I would like to be present, wherever parents are crying for their children I want to be present to console, care, aid, and serve. With my meager forces and the aid of God. Please be assured that I carry you both in my heart, wherever you are, and wherever I am. We are, we remain, Jeannette, Clara, Charles, and myself one family, the Spodek family. May the grace of God appease your immense suffering and bring you consolation, strength, and courage. I know that you do not lack them, that you never lacked them.

> Your daughter who loves you,
> Sister Maria Teresa

P.S. You can continue to write to me via Sister Marie-Paule, our Mother Superior, who faithfully transmits your letters, which I always read with infinite sadness and very great happiness.

(In the evening, in the Spodek home, the radio is on, the June 44 Company is performing a tragedy. Charles and Clara are seated at a table, and in silence, they are eating. Charles glances at the newspaper near his plate. Clara makes a gesture toward her breast. Charles looks up, and Clara stops her gesture. Charles eats, then:)

CHARLES: If you want to reread it, go into the bedroom.

CLARA: Read what?

CHARLES: Go into the bedroom.

CLARA: I'm eating, if you don't mind. *(Silence)* He reads at the table, and I . . .

(Silence, She remains for a moment forcing herself to eat calmly, then suddenly she pushes away her plate, draws herself up, and goes off to the bedroom. Then Charles gently pushes away his plate and places the newspaper directly in front of him. From the radio, the June 44 Company continues to perform the tragedy. Blackout.)

Scene 11: The Moroccan

(At breakfast.)

CLARA: We just received a letter.

CHARLES: Another one?

CLARA: A letter from Gisèle.

CHARLES: Gisèle? What Gisèle?

CLARA: Gisèle de Toulouse.

CHARLES: Gisèle de Toulouse?

CLARA: The one who's in Israel.

CHARLES: Then why are you saying from Toulouse?

CLARA: I'm not talking about Toulouse, I'm talking about my cousin, Gisèle. We called her Gisèle de Toulouse to distinguish her from my two other cousins with the same name who weren't from Toulouse and who were taken away.

CHARLES: There's only one Gisèle left?

CLARA: Yes, the one from Toulouse. She lives in Israel. (*Silence*) Why stay here, Charles? What's holding us back? (*A short silence*) Now that the Jews have a country . . .

CHARLES: I already have a country, and I've already had problems with it, thank you.

CLARA: Charles . . .

CHARLES: Where would I go, and what would I do over there?

CLARA: Just what you do here.

CHARLES: Just like that! I'll go and set myself up in a country where there are more dentists than holes in their teeth.

CLARA: Why do you say that?

CHARLES: A country for Jews is inevitably packed with doctors and dentists.

CLARA: Sick people, too, Charles, above all, sick people. They come from all over the world with their illnesses, their sufferings, their pain, their teeth, too.

(*Charles finishes his breakfast. He re-opens his newspaper. Silence.*)

CLARA: You've already read it. It's yesterday's.

(*He lowers the newspaper and stares at her.*)

CHARLES: So what?

CLARA: Well, I heard about a young woman who arrived from Morocco.

CHARLES: A Moroccan?

CLARA: No, one of us.

CHARLES: What's this "one of us"?

CLARA: Jewish.

CHARLES: An Ashkenaz?[15]

CLARA: No, a Jew from there.

CHARLES: From where?

CLARA: From Morocco!

CHARLES: So?

CLARA: So what?

CHARLES: What does it have to do with Gisèle de Toulouse?

CLARA: She's looking for a dentist's office.

CHARLES: Who's looking for a dentist's office?

CLARA: This Moroccan.

CHARLES: Tell her to go settle in Israel.

CLARA: I don't know her.

CHARLES: Then why are you telling me about her?

CLARA: She wants to settle in Paris.

CHARLES: I understand that. She's not doing well in Morocco?

CLARA: She's already left.

CHARLES: There are no more rotten teeth in Morocco?

CLARA: All of her patients have left Morocco.

CHARLES: For what grand purpose?

CLARA: Do I know? You read *Le Monde* day and night, not me.

CHARLES: The obituary pages mainly.

CLARA: The patients left, so she left, too.

CHARLES: She's wrong and the patients, too.

CLARA: Why is she wrong?

CHARLES: The Third World War will be less terrible there than here.

CLARA: Too bad for her, too late, she's here already. She's looking to move in, take over a practice, I mean . . .

CHARLES: Say no more. I see.

---

15. Ashkenazic Jews are mainly European Jews. The Sephardim are the Jews who were expelled from Spain in 1492 and who traveled over the Mediterranean Sea to settle in the lands along its shores. Many settled in Morocco, where an earlier migration of Jews already existed. They are all considered Sephardim.

CLARA: I thought . . .

CHARLES: What good does it do you to think?

(*Silence.*)

CLARA: I can't stand being here any more. I pass a nun and my legs go limp and I have palpitations for hours. And I haven't said anything about seeing cops, special police, and even neighbors in the building, it makes me . . .

(*She sighs. Charles reads the newspaper in silence. Clara cleans the table. Buzzer. Ringing at the door. The first patient has arrived. Charles gets up, slips on his white gown. Clara trots off to the door.*)

THE CHORUS: At last, thanks to Clara's stubbornness, the playwright, now fourteen years, three months old, met once a week with a brunette with an accent who moved about with a breast full of good humor, who dressed both in winter and in summer in a pink smock with short sleeves, who never bit her lips, and—above all, the very best part—who broke out laughing at the least word that Jean-Claude gargled forth. Often, and especially when she was dealing with the back teeth, the wisdom teeth, she had to brush by or even lean directly on one of Jean-Claude's arms, and she did this with the most striking part of her pink smock. Jean-Claude didn't budge for fear of losing contact. He ceased to be preoccupied by pain and fear, he concentrated on the inexplicable warmth that ended by setting ablaze another part of his anatomy. And what Spodek had not obtained with sermons and menaces, the smock of the Moroccan obtained quickly. Jean-Claude got into the habit of scrubbing his teeth intensely, especially when he had to go to his weekly rendezvous. Without Clara's being there anymore, Suzanne, without being asked by Jean-Claude, gave up accompanying him. However, Jean-Claude demanded long pants, instead.

SUZANNE: Long pants to go to the dentist? What next?

JEAN-CLAUDE: Can you see me seated in shorts with my leg in the air?

SUZANNE: You didn't make such a fuss with Spodek.

JEAN-CLAUDE: An apprentice can't go about everywhere in shorts.
SUZANNE: Why not?
JEAN-CLAUDE: It makes a bad impression.
SUZANNE: What makes a bad impression?
JEAN-CLAUDE: People can see my knees.
SUZANNE: So what, people can see mine!
JEAN-CLAUDE: I want long pants.
SUZANNE: Put on your golf pants, the one I bought you for your brother's bar mitzvah.
JEAN-CLAUDE: And look like a delivery boy on a bicycle? No thanks!
THE CHORUS: He got his long pants, and for decades he'd consider the smock with short sleeves the most troubling erotic accessory of feminine dress.

Scene 12: Stalingrad[16]

(*M. de Stalingrad is seated in the dentist's chair, his mouth wide open, while Charles works on his teeth.*)
CHARLES: (*Drawing back*) Spit.
(*Stalingrad spits and then immediately:*)
STALINGRAD: And what's to become of me?
CHARLES: There are other dentists between Stalingrad and Château-Rouge.
STALINGRAD: With whom I can talk the way I talk with you? Dentists who know what life is, suffering, Yiddishkeyt . . .
(*Charles interrupts him with the drill. Stalingrad picks up again.*)
STALINGRAD: All the dentists I know except you are Zionists, and who'd expect you, of all people, to give up first and set off for over there?

16. Stalingrad is a métro station on Line 2 at the border of the 10th and 19th arrondissements of eastern Paris. This quarter was heavily Jewish, mainly working-class Jewish immigrants who came around 1900. Today it is mainly African.

(*Charles leans once again over Stalingrad's mouth. Noise of the drill.*)

CHARLES: Spit.

(*Stalingrad spits heartily.*)

STALINGRAD: Do you know why they should never have made a Jewish state with borders and all?

(*Charles is busy mixing his dental compound. Stalingrad to his back:*)

STALINGRAD: We Jews, I do not know if you noticed, have many enemies, we have an enormous number of enemies all the time, but there is one type of enemy that we've never had: hereditary enemies across the border. Now as you see, we barely get a country with borders and we already have enemies at the borders, without having lost a single one of our old enemies. Believe me, Zionism is like communism; it's fine to be a communist or a Zionist in France as long as France doesn't itself become Zionist or communist, you get my drift.

CHARLES: (*Waiting*) Shut your trap and open your mouth wide![17]

STALINGRAD: There, there, what other dentist would dare talk to me like that? Just like my mother used to say to me when she wanted me to eat: shut your trap and open your mouth! That's exactly what she said . . .

(*Charles comes closer, a gouge and dental compound in hand. Stalingrad stops talking. Charles rummages about and then stops.*)

STALINGRAD: I should spit?

CHARLES: No, don't move. (*He fusses.*) There.

STALINGRAD: Should I spit?

CHARLES: No, clench your teeth tight.

STALINGRAD: (*Continuing to speak while clenching his teeth*) It's not a country we need, it's simply another planet! Another planet in another galaxy! You see, our problem . . .

CHARLES: Spit. (*Stalingrad spits. Charles raises the dentist's seat.*) All done, finished.

(*Stalingrad descends from the seat and brushes himself off, then:*)

---

17. From the Yiddish, "Farmakh dem pisk un efn dayn moyl!" (In French, "Ferme ta gueule et ouvre ta bouche!")

STALINGRAD: So this is the end of the game?

(*Charles nods. Stalingrad pays him, then puts out his hand. Charles ex-tends his own. Stalingrad suddenly falls into his arms, embracing him, murmuring . . .*)

STALINGRAD: I'm gonna miss you, I'm gonna miss you terribly. The deportee's wife, with whom I'm living, speaks only of her ex and of her ex-children. I told her: Me, too, I also lost a wife, children, parents. . . . Excuse me, can I spit once more?

CHARLES: (*Offering him his hat while Stalingrad spits*) You know the of-fice has been taken over . . .

STALINGRAD: . . . by a woman, I know, I know, your wife told me. Do you really see me coming here to talk about my life to a young woman who's just arrived from the Sahara?

CHARLES: But to take care of your teeth?

STALINGRAD: What's wrong with my teeth? (*He takes his hat.*) No, no, there are very good dentists near where I live, don't worry about me, worry more about yourself and Mrs. Clara. Still, one last joke for the road . . .

(*Buzzer!*)

CHARLES: So sorry, someone's waiting for me.

STALINGRAD: You have a waiting room, don't you? It's the moment to clear the deck.

CHARLES: I don't like to hear jokes or making my patients wait.

STALINGRAD: Monsieur Charles, for each one of his misfortunes, man has to make a little joke to tell at the end of a meal, that is a mitzvah.

(*Clara appears furtively and murmurs:*)

CLARA: Charles, the Moroccan is here . . .

CHARLES: (*To Stalingrad, in a low voice like his*) The legitimate usurper has just arrived to carry off the throne. Do you want me to in-troduce you?

(*Stalingrad quickly shakes his head as he moves to the exit, and also in a low voice:*)

STALINGRAD: A very short one then, on the run, you say to me Sha-lom, I answer you Rabinowitz! (*He laughs.*) Now you can laugh, Monsieur Charles. That's the end of the joke.

CHARLES: (*Serious as the pope*) I don't get it, but I'll laugh.
(*Silence. Stalingrad approves gravely. Then, still in a low voice:*)
STALINGRAD: The world prefers laughter to tears, what can you do?
We have to adapt, right?
(*Blackout.*)

Scene 13: Ship at Sea

(*The dentist's torture chair and apartment have disappeared with the departure of the Spodeks. Charles and Clara are in a minuscule cabin off to the Promised Land. Two bunks, a tiny washbasin, their luggage piled up in a heap. The ship is moving. The wind and the roar of the waves are heard.*)
CHARLES: Why does it rock like this?
CLARA: We're at sea, Charles.
CHARLES: Thank you, thank you very much for the information, it's a real pleasure to travel with a guide like you.
CLARA: (*Singing*)

> A boat on the water
> The river, the river
> A boat on the water
> Fell in the water
> Plop

(*Charles feels like vomiting.*)
CLARA: Something wrong?
CHARLES: Only this wretched taste in my mouth . . .
CLARA: Do you remember that boat ride on the Rhine?
CHARLES: I must have eaten something rotten.
CLARA: I ate the same thing you did.
CHARLES: So, so what, what does that prove?
(*A pause.*)
CLARA: You were afraid the kids would get seasick.
CHARLES: The Rhine sickness!
CLARA: In the end, you caught it. I had to hold your head up during the entire end of the boat ride while at the same time I was

combing their Alsatian dolls and playing catch with . . . (*She stops. Silence. He retches.*) What are you saying?

CHARLES: I'm talking to myself.

CLARA: And what are you saying inside?

CHARLES: I'm chewing myself out.

CLARA: About what?

CHARLES: (*After a hesitation*) Because of love, I have to abandon my house, my country, my street, my language. . . . We'll have to speak—what language over there?

CLARA: Hebrew.

CHARLES: There!

CLARA: What there?

CHARLES: Hebrew for me is Hebrew!

CLARA: We'll pick it up quickly.

CHARLES: I already know how to groan in Hebrew!

CLARA: They give courses as soon as you arrive.

(*He retches again and presses his hands on his mouth. Clara makes a move toward him.*)

CHARLES: (*Pushing her away*) Stop! It has to come out, everything has to come out! They need a new man for their new country!

CLARA: Gisèle will help us, too. (*He is twisting in pain, hanging over the washbasin, nothing comes out.*) And if you stick your fingers down your mouth?

(*Charles shakes his head.*)

CLARA: Do you think you have a fever?

CHARLES: No. Why?

CLARA: Do you have a headache?

CHARLES: Ask me where it doesn't hurt, then we'll gain some time.

CLARA: Charles . . .

CHARLES: Yes, what?

CLARA: And the photos?

CHARLES: What are you talking about?

CLARA: The photos, our photos, our photo albums?

CHARLES: In the storage room.

CLARA: In the storage room?

CHARLES: With the books, odds and ends, toys, the . . .

CLARA: All our souvenirs are in the storage room?

CHARLES: Too heavy to drag along.

CLARA: We agreed to keep the photos, didn't we?

(Silence.)

CHARLES: If they'd had a place for me, I would have gladly been deposited at Calberson's, with all the rest of the junk.

(The canticle breaks out suddenly, they listen to it for a moment, then . . .)

CHARLES: What's going on now?

CLARA: You hear it, too?

CHARLES: I hear it too well.

CLARA: Then it's not only in my head?

CHARLES: No, it's in mine too.

(They hear the words of the canticle. Then . . .)

CHARLES: Go look.

CLARA: Me?

CHARLES: Who else?

CLARA: All by myself?

CHARLES: I can't drag myself off, Clara, I really can't. *(He has another attack of retching.)* You see!

(The canticle increases in sound. Clara exits, staggering. The door remains open but bangs and bangs again from the wind. The canticle invades the stage. Charles moves his lips, shaping the words between two bouts of retching. Suddenly he runs to the basin and vomits beside it. Clara returns, haggard.)

CLARA: Charles, its horrible.

CHARLES: Yes, it's disgusting, but at least it's out of my system.

CLARA: Nuns, nuns all over the place on the deck, and they're singing and singing, if you only knew!

CHARLES: Give me a rag.

CLARA: What?

CHARLES: Any old rag. Where are they going?

CLARA: To their holy places.

CHARLES: What holy places?

CLARA: Over there, in our homeland.

(Charles wipes, wipes the ground, then sits and laughs.)

CLARA: What are you laughing at?

CHARLES: Tales of the good Sisters always make me laugh.

CLARA: It's enough to make you tear your hair out. They're singing, they're laughing, and some of them are dancing in a circle.

CHARLES: It seems to be rocking less.

CLARA: It's rocking just as much, but you're getting used to it.

CHARLES: You get used to everything or nearly . . .

(*Suddenly a Hassidic song is heard. The canticles blur. Charles and Clara, seated, listen. The songs get louder.*)

CLARA: They sing well.

(*Charles looks at her, says nothing, then spreads out.*)

CLARA: I'm going to see them.

CHARLES: Who?

CLARA: Ours!

CHARLES: If you find a *Le Monde* by any chance, I miss the obituaries already.

CLARA: Soon you'll read your own obituary, in Hebrew.

CHARLES: Let's hope so.

CLARA: Fine, I'm going upstairs.

CHARLES: All right, but don't catch cold!

(*She is already beyond the door. The door bangs and opens again. Charles gets up and unsteadily goes to shut the door.*
Blackout.)

Epilogue

(*The canticles and the Hassidic songs become prayers as the Chorus appears . . .*)

THE CHORUS: Well, here we are, the time has come to leave the Spodeks, they're sailing to you, the Promised Land. They're sailing, ignorant of the promised country, they're sailing in between inherited diseases and modern seasickness. Soon the ship will have gone past Cyprus, having stopped for a short call, and will cast off for the Promised Land.

CLARA: (*Calling, from Off Stage*) Charles! Charles! Come up here! Come up here! We can see the coast!

(*Charles pulls himself up from the bunk.*)

CLARA: (*Appearing at the door of the cabin*) Hurry up, you'll miss it all! (*She leaves. Charles dresses. The canticle and the prayers build in intensity. Clara reappears.*)

CLARA: Put on your sunglasses and your straw hat! We're hugging the coastline. It's magnificent.

CHARLES: (*Placing his straw hat on his head while taking out his sunglasses.*) I suddenly do feel lighter.

(*Charles puts on his sunglasses and leaves, groping his way with an unsteady step.*)

THE CHORUS: If the production is well endowed—which the author fervently hopes—and if the setting allows for it, we could see projected high up in the theatre, in a brilliant though artificial sunset, Clara and Charles discovering their Promised Land, lost in an endless mass of devotees to a new life, standing shoulder to shoulder with nuns, priests, popes, and pastors in the dress of pilgrims, all locked in emotion, faith, and hope. Otherwise we must be content with uniting the dark with silence, unless the distant call of a muezzin suddenly pricks up our ears.[18]

---

18. The printed edition concludes the epilogue with the final Chorus of One announcing in comic grandiloquence how Clara and Charles and the other pilgrims stare in revery at the brilliant setting sun above their Promised Land. But in the first production at the Théâtre du Rond-Point in Paris and in subsequent productions, the final voice of the chorus becomes a voice-over, and only Clara and Charles on stage are staring out from the ship deck. They appear fervent as the stage lights begin to dim and the ship's horns blast twice, announcing its arrival at Haifa, Israel's major port city, with a substantial Arab presence clustered at the docks. At this point, as the stage lights begin to continually dim, one hears a muezzin's voice calling the faithful to prayer as Clara and Charles stare out in odd wonderment. The dimming stage lights then go out rapidly as the curtain falls sharply and intently, like a knife thrust. At the performance of the play I attended with the playwright, the audience laughed at the comic irony, fully comprehending the authorial position that I had heard Grumberg often repeat to me about this play and life: there are no Promised Lands, it is a utopic ideal.

FINIS

TOWARD YOU, PROMISED LAND

Canticle:

The people of God who are dragging themselves across the
   immense desert
Have fled slavery and hate: they are moving under a
   clear sky.
They are heading toward a distant land that God promised
   their ancestors
Where all distress will be cured in a calm and serene
   world.

Refrain:

Toward You, Promised Land,
The people of God extend their hand.
Toward You, Promised Land.
They turn their heart and their faith.
Toward You Promised Land,
They march despite conflict
Toward You, Promised Land, Toward You!

Canticle:

Bent under the weight of misery, all peoples are
   walking, too;
They are seeking joy, light; they are thirsty for an infinite
   world.
Where, then, is the Promised Land that does not deceive
   their hope?
Yes, it is their entrance into the Church that they pursue
   without knowing it.
The chains of the old enslavement are broken by our
   Savior,
And we pursue this journey toward another better world.
The sky is the eternal earth where death will introduce us
If we, faithful, know how to follow The Lord who will open
   it to us.

Mama's Coming Back, Poor Orphan

[*Maman revient, pauvre orphelin*]

The text is based on the Actes-Sud edition, 1994. The play was first performed in 1993 in a radio broadcast offered by France Culture (Radio France) in a program directed by Lucien Attoun, "The New Dramatic Repertory." It was first performed on stage in 1994 in Paris at the Théâtre du Vieux Colombier in a production directed by Philippe Adrien with the troupe of the Comédie Française.

—Mama, Mama, Where are you? Ma, Ma, I'm sick, Ma, aren't you in your favorite chair? She's not in her armchair. Your TV's not on? Her TV's not on. Not even the radio? Mama, where are you? Ma, Ma?

—Why are you shouting?

—I'm looking for Mama.

—Your mama's no longer there.

—Where is she?

—On my right.

—On your right?

—On my right.

—Who are YOU? Why don't I see you?

—Because.

—Because why?

—Because I am God.

—God?

—God!

—God.

—Then you exist?

—As you see.

—Then I've been mistaken all my life?

—What do you mean by that?

—I believed you didn't exist.

—The important thing was to believe.

—I was wrong the others were right.

—It's not because you were wrong that the others were right.

—Tell me.

—What?

—What type of God are you?

—A God among the gods who attempts to do his best but who can do little and, alas, does even less still.

—You're not quite God then?

—I am your God, let's say your private God.

—Ah . . .

—Make a wish.

—A wish?

—Yes, what do you want most?

—To see Mama again.

—All right. Sit down and wait. Be good. Mama's coming back, poor orphan.

—Mama, is it you?

—Who else should it be?

—You're coming back from shopping?

—Where else should I come from?

—Do you have something for me?

—Whom else should it be for?

—What is it?

—Potatoes, flour, salt, sugar, spaghetti, pasta shells.

—Yum, yum.

—Stand up straight.

—Mama?

—Mama's tired. Eat correctly!

—Mama?

—Did you wet your pants?

—Mama?

—Don't put your elbows on the table! Or your hands!

—Mama?

—Did you do your homework? The small errand? The big one? Go to bed! Sleep!

—Mama?

—Do things with both hands!

—Mama?

—With two hands! Use your right hand, your right hand!

—Mama?

—Don't run! Stay seated! You're going to dirty your clothes! You're going to fall!

—Mama?

—Did you put on your scarf, your beret, your hooded cape, your rabbit fur insoles?

—Mama?

—Mama's worn out. Straighten up! Lick the plate clean! Stand up straight! What will the neighbors say?

—Mama?

—What will the neighbors say?

—Mama?

—Stop shouting!

—Mama?

—Don't cry!

—Mama?

—Don't move!

—Mama, the lady at school said I had to take pills.

—What lady?

—The lady who came. She touched me there, and she said there was only one.

—What am I getting mixed up in? Who's this lady who dares touch you there?

—They call her doctor, Mama, from the Red Cross. She's going to write you about the pills. The sack on one side is empty she said. Only one has come down. The pills will make the other one come down. They'll fall into place and then it will be complete.

—It's the Red Cross that says that you've only one?

—Mama, there are three in the class who have only one. The teacher said it's tied to what we went through during the war. There's one person the pills won't help, and they'll have to operate on him, she said, according to the Red Cross, he suffered that badly during the war. And worse, I've got to wear braces on my teeth, a hernia support, eyeglasses, and insteps because my feet are turning inward . . .

—Shut up! Shut up! Shut up!

—God! God ! God! Something's not right!

—What, what? What's not going right?

—My Mother, this isn't my Mother!

—Just what's not going right, tell me?

—Who are you? God?

—I am the anesthetist, your anesthetist. How's your heart, your liver, your blood, your bronchial tubes, your lungs? They're doing fine, no?

—What are you going to do to me?

—We're going to operate on you, my dear little man.

—But since the Red Cross doctor said that the pills were enough . . .

—I don't know Doctor Cross . . .

—Red . . .

—Your case, dare we say, if not beyond hope, is well beyond solving by pills, believe me.

—But since the doctor . . .

—Cross, red or blue, is not in this department. We're going to try to inflate it with silicon, then we'll plug it with a laser before removing the silicon and then re-inflate it with gas, and then we'll seal it definitively. You see, the trouble is ours! You just have to rest stretched out on your stomach, Grandpa.

—No, no, God!

—God?

—Yes, God! I want to see God! Just a while ago I made a vow but it hasn't worked out.

—You didn't get hold of more analgesics, or even barbiturates? I'll have them pump out your stomach!

—No no, He came.

—Who?

—God.

—You saw Him?

—No, I heard His voice.

—You heard His voice?

—Just as I hear yours. I wanted to see Mama again, but not the one I just saw, not the evil one.

—A mother is never evil.

—This one was evil.

—No, no. she was afraid, no doubt.

—Afraid?

—Afraid.

—Of what?

—Of everything. Afraid for you, your case is quasi-hopeless. Besides, an operation like this, at your age, could quite properly frighten a mother who, if I'm not mistaken, and according to the most basic rules of calculation, is probably no spring chicken.

—Exactly. I want to see her again seated in her armchair in front of the TV.

—Fine, fine, I'll see what I can do. I'm going to transmit it to the highest echelon. Just rest there and remain calm. Mama's coming back, poor orphan.

—Mama, Mama! You're watching the TV without sound? Mama put on your hearing aid! Mama put on your hearing aid! Hello, Hello! I'm here, Mama! Get your hearing aid on! Mama!

—Ah, it's you?

—Your hearing aid!

—It buzzes.

—Fix it.

—There are no more batteries.

—If there had been more batteries, it wouldn't buzz so.

—You haven't bought me any batteries.

—Put your two hands down! Order, order, now! Posture! Pull yourself up! You're going to fall from your armchair! What! You
want me to turn on the sound?

—For something worthwhile!

—Did you see me last night?

—Did you come by last night?

—No, on TV, did you see me?

—No.

—But I told you, Ma, on Tuesday.

—You came by Tuesday?

—No, Sunday. I told you, there's a talk show on Tuesday.

—Oh yes, I must have seen the beginning of the discussion.

—I spoke at the end, Mama.

—I don't like talk shows.

—But I had told you, Mama, that I was speaking in that one.

—When?

—Sunday.

—Sunday there was a talk show?

—No, yesterday, Tuesday. I spoke in the talk show.

—About what?

—I'll explain it to you, Mama.

—What did you talk about?

—In fact, about all we suffered during the war, Mama.

—About all I suffered.

—But I was there, Mama, I was there, too.

—You were a baby.

—Babies suffered, too, Mama, babies suffered, too, I feel pain,
Mama, I feel pain all over.

—Sunday?

—Not Sunday, Tuesday.

—You're not coming Sunday?

—Yes, Mama, I'll come Sunday.

—On Sunday they always serve rabbit in mustard sauce.

—At home, on Sunday it was chicken we had roasted at the bakery with potatoes and onions in gravy.

—Yes.

—You remember?

—Ask them.

—What do you want me to ask them Mama?

—For some roast chicken on Sunday instead of rabbit in mustard sauce.

—I'll ask them.

—Good.

—But rabbit in mustard sauce is delicious, Mama, a real French specialty.

—I don't like it. I hate it.

—Maybe theirs isn't good?

—I don't know, I never tasted it. I wouldn't taste rabbit in mustard sauce for anything in the world, I don't like such things, I'm telling you.

—Did Papa like it?

—Papa? Your father or my father?

—My father, Mama, Papa.

—Did he like what?

—Rabbit in mustard sauce, Mama?

—How should I know? We never ate any. I already hated it. He liked roasted chicken and kasha,[1] that he liked.

—What's kasha?

—You wouldn't like it.

---

1. Kasha is a cereal dish made of buckwheat groats that have been sautéed or roasted and then boiled. It was the poor man's food in eastern Europe, particularly in Russia and the Ukraine. The Jews there ate it constantly. The main difference was in preparation in that Gentiles used lard to sauté the groats while the Jews used rendered chicken or goose fat instead—a matter of Jewish dietary laws—*kashrut*. Rabbit is not a kosher animal that can be consumed.

—What is it?

—He liked to drink a round with his buddies on Sundays, that's how it was. On Sunday, the only thing that counted for him was being with his buddies.

—Who were his buddies?

—Do I know? Buddies.

—Buddies or friends?

—Gambling friends, yes.

—He was a gambler?

—With his friends, yes.

—But all the same, you got along well?

—Who?

—Papa and you?

—We were married.

—I know that, Mama, really.

—We were, as they say, husband and wife. And then after . . .

—I know all about after, Mama. But how was it before?

—Before what?

—Before after, Mama.

—You're confusing me.

—Sit up straight, don't slump and don't blink your eyes like that!

—My eyes are closing on me.

—Are you sleepy?

—No, my eyes are closing. I can't shut them at nighttime but during the day they close all by themselves.

—You're sleepy.

—No.

—Why is your leg moving?

—Is it?

—Stop moving your legs like that, Mama!

—It's not me that's moving them.

—Do you want to take a little walk?

—What time is it?

—Do you want to go out? Take a walk around the garden?

—It's too late.

—It's still daytime.

—There's a chill in the air. You came too late.

—I come when I can, Mama.

—If you came today, it's because you won't come on Sunday.

—I shall come Sunday!

—Why are you shouting?

—I'm not shouting.

—If you can't come you can't come, it makes no difference.

—I come every Sunday.

—Not every Sunday!

—Not every Sunday.

—Almost all, Mama! Almost all!

—I like it best when you come on Sunday.

—I come on Sundays, Mama.

—It's not the same thing during the week.

—I come every week on Sunday and on Tuesday.

—Is today Tuesday?

—No, Wednesday. Yesterday was Tuesday.

—You came yesterday?

—No, I said I had the talk show.

—Said?

—What?

—Are you earning a living?

—Am I earning a living?

—You make a living telling about how I suffered?

—No, I live by begging. I'll end up on the scaffold!

—You see, during the week you get all worked up. On Sunday
  you're calmer.

—I write books, Mama! I write books!

—Don't shout, so you write books, I know.

—"Don't shout! What are the neighbors going to think?" They're
  deaf here, the neighbors, Mama. Everyone's deaf here. I can
  shout as much as I want!

—Who's interested in them?

—What Mama, what?

—The books you write?

—I don't know Mama, it depends.

—Who's interested in what other people have suffered? Everyone's suffered.

—That's why there are so many potential readers, Mama! It creates a lot of clients, all this suffering, Mama!

—I wouldn't like to read such sad things.

—Wouldn't you be afraid of crying?

—I don't cry anymore. Nothing makes me cry now. Why should I?

—I don't know. Before you cried all the time.

—That's over. I don't cry any more. Why would I cry? If I read, I'd read love stories. That's it.

—I'm sorry, but I haven't written any love stories, Mama.

—You should. That's what people want to read!

—Well, look who's here! The famous writer! And how does she look today?

—Quite well, Monsieur Director. Thank you.

—Tell him . . .

—Tell him what?

—About the rabbit . . .

—You want to know something? Yesterday my son, he's a real fan of yours, saw you at the beginning of the talk show.

—I was at the end.

—You were very good.

—You saw me?

—No, my own son. He's a fan. Do you know that we can no longer take care of her.

—Tell him . . .

—She makes up allergies to her heart's content. Have you shown him your pimples?

—Tell him about the chicken . . .

—She comes up with pimples, eczema, blotches, and breaks in the skin. And then she no longer wants to walk, tell her . . .

—Tell him on Sunday . . .

—If she no longer walks she's going to find herself paralyzed. And
   then her bodily functions, she's a bit careless, you know, in her
   functions . . .

—Tell him on Sunday chicken, not rabbit!

—No, no, no! Enough! Let's just drop it!

—My dear young sir, you seem a bit agitated . . .

—It's Mama, she's bothering me. Who are you?

—Still the anesthetist. You're in the recovery room.

—The operation took place?

—The first one, yes.

—And God?

—God, my God, has other fish to fry, I suppose . . .

—Tell him, tell him, I want to spend a Sunday, a really enjoyable
   Sunday with Mama.

—Take it easy. Build up your spirits. Everything went well. Remain
   on your stomach, the surgeon's very happy.

—I can see him?

—He's already left.

—Where to?

—For his weekend. It was a stroke of luck that he came by to operate on you at the end of the week!

—God, I am speaking to you of God, I want to see God again!

—Your tablets.

—I'm allergic.

—To what?

—Anything in great quantities.

—Then nothing in great quantities, there, written down in large
   letters, nothing in great quantities! Now take a rest, relax!

—Say to God: Have a happy Sunday!

—Sh! Be good . . . Mama's coming back, poor orphan.

—Mama, is it you?

—It's me.

—It's Sunday?

—It's Sunday.

—What are we going to do this Sunday?

—Some roast chicken.

—No, besides that, what shall we do?

—We'll go visit Grandpa.

—Every Sunday?

—Yes.

—Why every Sunday?

—He's sick, he's old, he's all alone.

—And after, what will we do?

—We'll go eat your favorite pastry.

—And then?

—Go to the movies.

—Great! And see what?

—Whatever's playing.

—A Laurel and Hardy?

—If it's playing.

—Mama?

—Yes?

—Which one's the fat one?

—Hardy.

—And the thin one?

—Laurel.

—I like Laurel, and you?

—I like him, too.

—And Charlie Chaplin, do you like him?

—I do.

—If there's a Charlie Chaplin and no Laurel and Hardy, will we go
    to Charlie Chaplin?

—We'll go to Charlie Chaplin.

—And what if there's no Charlie Chaplin and no Laurel and Hardy?

—We'll see whatever else there is.

—Like every Sunday, right?

—Like every Sunday.

—A romance?

—No, that's foolish.

—A cowboy and Indians and a character with a star?

—Yes, my love.

—Mama, Mama! I feel so bad, I'm so afraid! Why do I feel so bad? Why am I so afraid?

—As long as there is life, my darling, there's fear with a little pointed end that causes pain somewhere.

—So we're well?

—We are.

—We're back on our feet?

—We are.

—We lack nothing?

—Nothing.

—And the adenoids?

—That'll be another time, the adenoids.

—And Papa?

—Your papa or my papa?

—My papa! I'd like to see him once, Papa . . .

—Are we talking all alone?

—Is God still trailing along in the corridor?

—God? I thought you didn't believe in Him.

—What made you think that?

—I read your books.

—You?

—Me.

—And so?

—It's sad.

—What do you mean?

—To see that you, too, are beginning . . .

—I'm beginning to what?

—To believe in God.

—I don't believe more than that, He came to see me, that's all.

—When?

—Not long ago.

—I'm going to reduce the cortisone. It makes you high. Do you remember me?

—You're the anesthetist.

—No, I'm the internist, the director.

—What director?

—The home where your mother . . .

—Mama?

—I am the son of the director.

—Mama . . .

—I saw you on TV.

—You saw me?

—On the TV. I don't look at it much.

—What?

—TV. When I was young, I was a real fan.

—Mama . . .

—Those were the days.

—Those were the days.

—The garden was beautiful, wasn't it?

—The garden, oh yes.

—Go, take a rest, sweet dreams.

—Tell God that I'd like to see Papa at least once.

—I'll tell him, if I see him. Close your eyes. . . . Papa's coming
    back, poor orphan.

—Papa, is that you?

—Who do you want it to be?

—Why can't I see you?

—I can't be shown.

—Why?

—Too damaged.

—Damaged?

—Why are you hanging around in pajamas?

—I'm sick, Papa.

—At your age?

—I'm sixty-two, Papa!

—Already?

—And you?

—My pajamas aren't fit to wear anymore.

—No, how old are you?

—Forty-two.

—Forty-two?

—Forty-two plus one gold tooth.

—I have all my teeth Papa, but I no longer have a big appetite.

—Tell me, son.

—What, Papa?

—The truth.

—What truth?

—About people.

—Yes, Papa?

—Have people understood?

—Understood what, Papa?

—People no longer hunt down a stranger in the streets of gray cities?

—No, Papa.

—The worker works in joy, and each receives according to his needs?

—Yes, Papa.

—And children in the whole world have plenty to eat?

—Yes, Papa.

—And no longer tremble from bombing raids?

—No, Papa.

—No human being is discriminated against because of his birth or origin?

—No, Papa.

—Frontiers are abolished, nationalism is put down?

—Yes, Papa.

—Mankind no longer behaves like a wolf toward other men?

—No, Papa. . . . That is . . . yes, Papa.

—Well then, it's to us, to us that you owe it. To us the last victims of blind barbarity whose ashes are spread about to fertilize the Eastern plains, to us the sacrificed, the victims of police raids, the incinerated.

—Yes, Papa.

—Then why are you hanging around in pajamas? The world is
    yours. We bequeathed it to you.

—Yes, Papa, thank you, Papa.

—What type of job do you have?

—Papa, I'm retired.

—Sixty-two and already retired! We really did our job well.

—Before I was a writer, Papa.

—A writer?

—Yes, Papa, a writer.

—Enough to make a living?

—That's how I earned my living, Papa.

—In the *Daily Worker*?

—Not exactly, Papa.

—I would have liked to write about the life of the hardhats in the
    Farm Laborers Journal, but . . .

—Were you one of them?

—No, why?

—Tell me, Papa, what was it like between you and Mama?

—Who?

—Mama, my mother and you, what was it like?

—When?

—I don't know, Sunday . . .

—Sunday?

—Yes, on Sunday, what was it like?

—Well, you see, we were to put it simply husband and wife.

—I know that, Papa.

—And then there was . . .

—I know everything afterward, Papa, but before, before, what was
    it like?

—When?

—On Sundays, Papa.

—On Sunday I went to the café in the morning . . .

—With Mama?

—No, She was lukewarm on political matters.

—And in the afternoon?

—I went out to get a bit of fresh air in the afternoon.

—With Mama?

—No.

—Why not with Mama, Papa?

—She didn't like horse races. She went to see her father.

—And in the evening?

—I went to sleep. By nighttime . . . I was worn out.

—With Mama?

—We were husband and wife, I told you.

—But what was it like between you?

—Between us?

—Did you argue?

—We were . . .

—Husband and wife, I know Papa, I know!

—Why are you so nervous?

—I'm not nervous, Papa.

—Yes, you are nervous.

—It's the first time we're talking to each other!

—Whose fault is that?

—I don't know, Papa.

—Don't think about the past any more. Enjoy your life. Enjoy!

—I don't know, Papa.

—You don't know what?

—How to enjoy.

—Learn.

—At sixty-two?

—It's time, that's for sure.

—Papa, tell me, do you see Mama?

—Where?

—There where you are?

—Where I am?

—Yes, do you see her?

—She is where she is?

—At His right side.

—At the right side of whom, God?

—At His right side, Papa.

—Let's start again, at whose right side is she? Son?

—Of God, Papa.

—About whom are you talking?

—Papa, it was He who permitted you to come, wasn't it?

—It was you, you who called out for me, wasn't it?

—It was me, yes.

—As soon as you called for me, I came. If you'd called for me
   sooner, I would have come earlier.

—So that's how it works.

—That's how.

—Why do you have the same voice as He has?

—Who?

—You went to the movies?

—Who?

—And you liked kasha?

—When you're hungry . . . Life was hard, very hard, and if we
   didn't do everything to change it, it'd still be the same, and
   you'd be eating kasha.

—Papa?

—What?

—Why do I feel so bad? Why am I so afraid?

—You're not a bit of a whiner like your mother, are you?

—I don't know, Papa.

—Do you like horse races?

—I don't know, Papa.

—You don't know too much.

—I don't.

—Then listen: Forget the past, throw off your pajamas, get up and
   walk. Poor orphan, Mama and Papa will never come back!

(*Music.*)

TRANSLATED BY SETH L. WOLITZ[1]

An Interview with Jean-Claude Grumberg

Conducted by Anne Cassou-Nogues and Marie-Aude de Langenhagen

Q: What portion of the play, The Workplace, *draws on your personal experience?*

A: I think quite a large one—it's like placing an autobiography on stage. It means that the theatre requires a transposition. But the character of my mother [Simone] and her reality, the arrest of my father, everything Simone relates, and even the setting of the workplace—that is the very workplace where my mother worked and the workplaces where I myself worked, etc.—all these elements are autobiographical. Thus the play is directly tied to my life, but the ensemble is transposed by the requirements of theatrical form.

Q: Did you depend strictly on your memories, or did you do serious research in order to capture the ambiance of the post-war era?

A: The problem I had was the precise memories that I had to transform into short scenes.

Furthermore, I faced a major task collecting documentary evidence, for example, on the return of the deportees. It was extremely difficult to find documents for that time period when I was writing the play. The available documentation had to provide enough fodder for the actresses during our efforts at improvisation. I had, in fact,

---

1. This is a translation of the interview by Anne Cassou-Nogues and Marie-Aude de Langenhagen in Jean-Claude Grumberg, *L'Atelier* [original 1979 play] (Malesherbes: GF Flammarion, 2006), 5–23.

a big problem writing the first scene: as the character of Simone was my mother, I thought that her story should be foregrounded, but that didn't work out. It was Théâtre Ouvert[2] that suggested that I should work through improvisations with the actresses to find theatrical solutions.

From the very first days, I realized that Simone was just a character like any other who entered a workplace and that the central personage was the group. Much effort was thus expended to provide documentary evidence in order to nurture the improvisations. These improvisations permitted me to transform these overly precise memories or the overly precise documentary evidence into something more alive. The first and last scenes were born out of these improvisations, the other scenes were written out before beginning the improvisations.

Q: Into which characters have you placed the most of yourself?

A: There is of course the child at the end. And there is the boss, Leon.

Q: Because you played the role of Léon?

A: No! I ended up playing the role of Léon because the actors projected the image of an exploiting boss, a very tough guy, and I did not want that. He is a type of man who just seeks to live his life; he exploits himself first, with his wife. The verbal exchanges of the female workers must not be taken as truth. It is their truth, as the boss expresses his truth when he speaks of the women workers. I was trying therefore to render a sort of homage to these small businessmen/bosses in whose places I worked as an apprentice tailor, and they had a bunch of decent qualities. At the same time, he is an excessive character. But I placed a lot of myself into him.

---

2. Théâtre Ouvert (Open Theater) in Paris belongs to the Centre National des Dramaturgies Contemporaines (National Center of Contemporary Dramatic Arts), which provides performance space for and dramatic advice to new playwrights and showcases new works. Director Lucien Attoun has aided and introduced many contemporary French dramatists.

And, of course, there is the personage of my mother [Simone], whose role, oddly, I was perhaps most reticent to develop. And for that reason I wrote *Mama's Coming Back, Poor Orphan* [*Maman revient, pauvre orphelin*]. I was drawn back again to the evocation of my mother; there is something more intimate in this later text.

Therefore, the fact that Simone opens the play and that the play cannot continue without her is particularly significant. . . .

It's about retelling her life, and through her the disappearance of my father. Simone does not conclude the play; it is her absence that brings it closure.

Q: Why have you chosen to treat this painful subject? Is it driven by your personal experience (more than anyone else)? Do you feel committed to a "duty to remember"? Did current events motivate the creation of your play?

A: At the time of writing my play, the term "duty to remember" did not exist. I had just had a great success with a play called *Dreyfus*, and I said to myself, if I were a playwright, I should prove it to myself by telling a story others could not tell. I think that when you write, you should write what others cannot write.

Q: Did the writing of this play prove difficult?

A: Very difficult. Writing it took five years. And when I say five years—the writing of *Zone libre* [*The Free Zone*] took ten but I was writing for television, film, and also other theatre pieces—that is, five years without writing anything else. I did not write every day, of course, but I wrote a scene, then I stopped for several months.

The major difference between an ordinary piece of theatre and *The Workplace* is that generally the characters in plays appear to state things, to address the audience, whereas, in *The Workplace*, they come to work. They are people who come to earn their keep and who, by chance, speak. They speak of this and that. They say stupidities, they say important things, they confide in one another, they laugh, they cry. . . . But the essential element is that they work. The "main character" of the play, over and above my life, is the workplace. I was born in a workplace, my father worked in the apartment where we were living—even if I do not have memories of him working—we slept in the room that served him as a workplace, my mother worked in a workplace that was right next to the house. I was myself an apprentice tailor—I worked in eighteen places—and I married a woman who had a workplace. This setting, the workplace, is the principal actor. Of course, the actors are there to speak to the public, but there is something more concrete than usual, which is that one has to see them working, and you have to have the impression that they are not there to talk but for work, to earn their keep.

Q: Did the structure of the work emerge straight away?

A: The structure of the work resembles that of *Dreyfus* [1974] and *En r'venant de l'Expo* [1973], which are earlier plays, and even the structure of *Amorphe d'Ottenburg* [1971].

The gathering together of various scenes led progressively to the construction of the story line. It is the act of writing that creates the structure and not the reverse. The needs of the story line decide how the story is organized.

There were problems dealing with the choice of days and hours, the problem of the seasons and that of the time length, since the play stretches from 1945 to 1952. The interior of the scenes needed to be both very alive and yet permit the passage of time.

When I say that I worked on the play for five years, at times I wrote a scene in a quarter of an hour, but I was writing a scene every six months. And when it emerged, it emerged just like that.

Q: In what range of generic mode(s) do you place your play? Why do you resort often to the use of the comic to deal with this painful and grave subject?

A: The play can be placed in the tradition of Yiddish literature, always tied to drama and to daily life; very often, Yiddish literature lets you see ordinary people facing insoluble problems. Each time it is a question of producing laughter and tears from the same situation.

Let me say once more, I did not choose—I did not say to myself, "Look, I'm going to do something that is part of this tradition." It just emerges, a natural expression. As soon as I began to write, be it on this subject or another, drama and laughter are joined together. There is even a more prosaic reason: Imagine you invite a sick uncle for dinner who talks incessantly about his illness without making you laugh. You would not invite him again; it is too much to bear. Therefore, when you talk about your life, you must make people who are listening laugh.

Isn't there also a need for some lightness in order to thwart the pain? Even lightness is not enough, but on occasion real coarse humor. When you write, you have to amuse yourself. And to pay homage to the victims, I believe in showing them alive—showing them alive, and not just to mourn them.

Q: Where do you place this play in the totality of your works?

A: It is not I who gives the play a place; I believe it is the play that is performed everywhere and that continues to be performed, that is studied in certain classes and often performed by amateurs. I'm the author, as it were, of *The Workplace*, and I have written other plays.

This play has for me, of course, a special history because I performed in it, because it is the story of my mother. . . . There is *The Workplace*, and there is *Mama's Coming Back, Poor Orphan*, and *Mon père, Inventaire* [My father, an inventory], which is not a piece of theatre but a series of stories. In these texts, I have also spoken of my life, but transposing less and less.

Q: You are the author of a novel, La nuit tous les chats sont gris *[At night all cats are gray], but more significantly the author of over thirty plays. Why have you preferred the theatre?*

A: At the beginning of my career, I was an actor. I became an author by default: I didn't have any work as an actor, so I wrote plays to pass the time. I was a constant reader of literature, an obsessive reader of novels, short stories, of literature in general, but I never sought to measure myself against *Moby-Dick* of Melville, for example. . . . You are going to tell me what about Shakespeare and Molière. . . . It took me a while to accept myself as an actor, and then it took me a while to accept myself as an author. In other words, I was not destined to act or to write. With my first experiences acting, I felt myself closer to writing drama than writing fiction.

At present, I like more and more short forms—short stories. It is what appeals to me most, to succeed in saying the maximum with the least number of words possible. I wrote many short plays from the beginning of my career. I am rather moved and astonished to see plays written in the 1960s continue to be performed.

The difference between writing fiction and writing drama is that when you write a novel, you address your reader directly, if you have the luck of finding an editor who will publish you. If you write a piece of theatre, it must be performed to reach its public. Of course, it has a double goal: it can be read and performed. At the beginning of my career, I could not imagine that my plays would be published, so I wrote them only for performance. You are not an isolated person when you work in theatre; you accept this strange adventure, which is to write something very personal so that people whom you hardly know carry it off and present it to the public. If it pleases, you are a good author. If it does not please, you are a bad author. It is as if you were preparing to take an examination, but on the day of the examination, other people took your place. There is a sense of group feeling that, no doubt, my personality needs; I did not see myself doing something special writing, and I did not claim the title of author.

Q: Who are the dramatists to whom you feel close?

A: Before all else . . . I wish to insist on the fact that one cannot write without reading. It is because one is a reader that one can be a writer. I read Shakespeare, the great novels of Dostoyevsky, Balzac, Victor Hugo. . . . But those writers who touched me most were no doubt the authors who drew my attention to translations of Yiddish writers or Jewish Americans, like [Bernard] Malamud and Saul Bellow.

Among the dramatists, there was Chekhov, of course, Eugene O'Neill, and naturally Samuel Beckett. I think that Beckett opened the door to people like me. That is to say, that until Samuel Beckett and [Eugène] Ionesco—who, strangely, are, both of them, immigrants who chose the French language—playwrights wrote in a rather grandiloquent language for theatre.

It became a necessity at least to learn grammar, which I did not know and still do not know. This possibility of writing works that are not constructed in the classical [French] manner and with a rather limited vocabulary when all is said and done, we owe to Beckett and Ionesco. And they had to break with this past literature that had gone bankrupt during World War II.

Q: How do you define the work of the director?

A: In the ideal, the director is the interpreter of the author. At present we are watching an usurpation of power by the director who makes, quite often, the play become a pretext for the elaboration of his own work. But the work of directors is very ephemeral. The work of the dramatist has endurance that is tied to the writing and to the publication. The performed play becomes a work shared by author and director.

The director is the one who oversees the theatrical space and the meaning of the work. It is not because you read that you understand. You must have someone who is the guarantor of meaning. If a director stages Molière's *The Miser*, he has great freedom, but what he does not have in his freedom is to remake the miser into a very generous man. In the context of *The Miser*, there is rarely a mistaken interpretation. But if you take a play like *The Merchant of Venice*, with the personage of Shylock, you realize that you must control this figure and not let it become a caricature. *The Merchant of Venice* has served for a very long time as the banner for anti-Semitism on stage. In the same way, for *The Workplace*, you can imagine a director transforming Leon into a monster, by removing the distance that self-mockery and humor provide.

The director should be the guarantor of the word of the author as well as the one who "mothers" the actors. Of course, he has an artistic responsibility.

Q: Do you consider yourself an auteur engagé, *a committed writer [to some philosophical or ideological position], and do you think a writer should be* engagé *[committed]?*

A: When you address a public, you have a responsibility. You have to express yourself, not only to amuse people: You give an accounting of the world in which you live and stir the spectator and lose him caught between laughter and tears. I never felt myself very *engagé*. I don't have a philosophical background or an education; nevertheless, I aspire to *m'engager* [to commit myself], but to what?

Selected Bibliography

TEXTS USED FOR TRANSLATIONS

Grumberg, Jean-Claude. *L'Atelier* (Arles: Actes Sud, 1985).

———. *Maman revient, pauvre orphelin* (Arles: Actes Sud, 1994).

———. *Vers toi terre promise: Tragédie dentaire* (Arles: Actes Sud, 2006).

GENERAL READING

Azama, Michel, ed. *De Godot à Zucco, Anthologie des Auteurs Dramatiques de langue française, 1950–2000*, vol. 3, *Le Bruit Du Monde*, 23–26. Paris: Éditions Theatrales, 2004.

Bartfeld, Fernande, ed. "Le Théâtre Juif." *Perspectives: Revue de l'Université Hebraïque de Jérusalem*, no. 10 (August 2003). Jerusalem: Hebrew University Magnes Press.

Bradby, David. *Le Théâtre en France de 1968 à 2000*. Paris: Honoré Champion, 2007.

Cassou-Nogues, Anne, and Marie-Aude de Langenhagen, eds. Interview in Jean-Claude Grumberg, *L'Atelier* [original 1979 play], 5–23. Malesherbes: GF Flammarion, 2006.

Caune, Jean. "Le Théâtre de Grumberg: Un lien sensible entre passé et présent." Postface in Jean-Claude Grumberg, *Dreyfus, L'Atelier, Zone Libre*, 363–380. Arles: Actes Sud, 1990.

Curtis, Michael. *Verdict on Vichy: Power and Prejudice in the Vichy France Regime.* New York: Arcade Publishing, 2003.

Finburgh, Clare, and Carl Lavery, ed. and introduction. *Contemporary French Theatre and Performance*. Houndmills: Palgrave Macmillan, 2011.

Jackson, Julien. *France: The Dark Years, 1940–1944*. Oxford: Oxford University Press, 2001.

King, Robert L. "Psychic Numbing and Grumberg's *L'Atelier*." *Massachusetts Review* 26, no. 4 (1985): 580–594.

Nacache-Ruimi, Claudine. *Étude sur Jean-Claude Grumberg, "L'Atelier."* Paris: Ellipses, 2007.

Plunka, Gene A., *Holocaust Drama: The Theater of Atrocity*. New York: Cambridge University Press, 2009.

Pocknell, Brian. "Jean-Claude Grumberg's Holocaust Plays: Presenting the Jewish Experience." *Modern Drama* 41, no. 3 (Fall 1998): 299–311.

Schumacher, Claude, ed. *Staging the Holocaust: The Shoah in Drama and Performance*. Cambridge: Cambridge University Press, 1998.

Skloot, Robert, ed. and introduction. *Theatre of the Holocaust*. Madison: University of Wisconsin, 1982.

Turk, Edward Baron, *French Theater Today*. Iowa City: University of Iowa Press, 2011.

Wolitz, Seth L. "Holocaust Memory in the French-Jewish Theater of Jean-Claude Grumberg." In *Jews and Theater in an Intercultural Context*, ed. Edna Nahshon, 137–142. Leiden and Boston: Brill, 2012.

OTHER TRANSLATIONS OF *L'ATELIER*

Grumberg, Jean-Claude. "The Workroom." Trans. Tom Kempinski. Playscript. Performed at Oxford Playhouse, 1980, and New Theatre, London, 1981.

———. *The Workroom*. American version. Trans. Daniel A. Stein with Sara O'Connor. New York: Samuel French, 1982.

———. *The Free Zone / The Workroom*. Trans. Catherine Temerson. New York: Ubu Repertory Theater, 1993.